Positive Discipline
for Single Parents

Other Books in the Developing Capable People Series:

For information on lectures, seminars, and leadership training workshops with Jane Nelsen or Cheryl Erwin, call 1-800-879-0812.

Positive Discipline for Single Parents

A Practical Guide to Raising Children Who Are Responsible, Respectful, and Resourceful

Jane Nelsen
Cheryl Erwin
Carol Delzer

Prima Publishing
P.O.Box 1260BK
Rocklin, CA 95677
(916) 786-0426

© 1994 by Jane Nelsen, Cheryl Erwin, and Carol Delzer

All rights reserved. No part of this book may be reproduced or transmitted in any form or by any means, electronic or mechanical, including photocopying, recording, or by any information storage or retrieval system, without written permission from Prima Publishing, except for the inclusion of quotations in a review.

Production: Janis Paris, Bookman Productions
Copyediting: Judith Abrahms
Typography: Peter Hancik, EuroDesign
Interior Design: Paula Goldstein
Cover Design: The Dunlavey Studio, Sacramento

Library of Congress Cataloging-in-Publication Data

Nelsen, Jane.
    Positive discipline for single parents: a practical guide to raising children who are responsible, respectful, and resourceful / by Jane Nelsen, Cheryl Erwin, and Carol Delzer
       p. cm.
    Includes index.
    ISBN 1-55958-355-X
    1. Single parents.   2. Child rearing.   3. Parenting.
4. Discipline of children.   I. Erwin, Cheryl.   II. Delzer, Carol.
III. Title.
HQ759.915.N45   1993
649.1'0243—dc20   93-17738
                                             CIP

94 95 96 97 98 RRD 10 9 8 7 6 5 4 3 2 1

Printed in the United States of America

How to Order:
Single copies may be ordered from Prima Publishing, P.O. Box 1260BK, Rocklin, CA 95677; telephone (916) 786-0426. Quantity discounts are also available. On your letterhead, include information concerning the intended use of the books and the number of books you wish to purchase.

To Carol, who convinced me that single parents have special needs; and to Cheryl, who champions the vision that single-parent families are not broken families. Both are shining examples of single parents who are providing nurturing and empowering homes for their children.

—*Jane Nelsen*

To my son, Philip, who has brought me such joy, and to Tom, whose courage to change made this book possible.

—*Cheryl Erwin*

To my daughter Jessica for all her inspiration and to her father for his cooperation in helping me be a single parent.

—*Carol Delzer*

Contents

INTRODUCTION

Single Parenting: Where We Are and Where We're Going

Ask a group of single parents what it feels like to be a single parent and you're likely to be bombarded by emotional outbursts. "I feel overwhelmed," says one single mom. "Guilty," adds a single dad. And then the words come tumbling out, faster and faster—*isolated, exhausted, bitter, scared, insecure, vulnerable, lonely, depressed, anxious, deeply sad.*

There are many roads to becoming a single parent. Some become single through the death of a spouse. Some parents never marry at all, either by choice or because of abandonment. Some parents divorce. Whatever the reason, once you've reached that destination—once you find yourself a single parent—what then?

Being a single parent in this complex world of ours is a tremendous challenge. Single parenting is a kind of "parenting plus": you face all the everyday tasks of raising children, plus the problems of doing a job alone that was originally designed for two people. It takes time to heal when you've suffered a loss, and many single parents bear wounds that are still raw. Feelings of grief, hurt, and rejection can be overwhelming at times.

Parents are usually aware of their own feelings, but it sometimes surprises them that their children feel many of the same things. If a parent has died, children have their own grief. If they've only known one parent, they may wonder why the missing parent chose to leave. And if they've watched their parents divorce, regardless of the reason, children must learn to accept their new situation and come to terms with their own anger, confusion, and sense of abandonment.

Only time can heal the wound left by a spouse's or a parent's death, or by losing a parent or spouse through divorce. However, when divorced parents can work together in a friendly fashion for the good of the child, the trauma associated with the breakup of a marriage can be greatly reduced. Either way, a child must still learn to live in a family that doesn't meet society's expectations about what's "normal."

Single parenting can be an undeniably stressful way of life. Financial worries often seem insurmountable. Balancing a job, a home, adequate time with children, and time for oneself is a tricky task. Mention the words *social life* to many single parents and you're likely to get an incredulous snort. "What social life?" they ask. "Who has time?"

Single parents are frequently concerned about the effect this new life will have on their children. Are children harmed by growing up in a single-parent family? Will they have stable relationships themselves when they grow up? Can one parent provide everything a child needs to grow up healthy and whole? These questions plague every single parent from time to time.

In groups of single parents, however, when all the negative feelings have been exhaustively explored, an interesting thing begins to happen. "Wait a minute," one dad may say. "My home is a lot more peaceful now that we're on our own." Heads may begin to nod. Slowly an amazing truth is revealed: There are good things about being a single parent, too.

What, you may wonder, can possibly be good about being a single parent? Regardless of how you became one, you may discover strengths as a single parent that you didn't know you possessed when you had someone else to depend on. Many single parents find that they enjoy the lack of conflict in their homes without another parent to second-guess their decisions and actions. Single parents are frequently able to be more spontaneous, able to enjoy their children more. Some single parents find their new lifestyle liberating. They enjoy their independence, the new opportunities that arise, and the satisfaction that comes from meeting a challenge successfully. And it can be fun to feel open and available!

Children too can learn and grow in a single-parent home. It's tremendously empowering to learn that not only can you survive a trauma, you can learn from it. Children being raised by single parents have the opportunity to make a real contribution to their family and to learn a great deal about their own worth and abilities.

Gardeners tell us that without storm winds blowing against it occasionally, a tree will not develop a strong root system. It's the gusting of the wind that forces the tree to dig in, to sink its roots down deep, to take a firm hold and hang on. The famous cypress trees along the California coast have suffered the lashings of wind and storm, but they're firmly rooted in the rock, and they don't let go even in the strongest gale. Their beauty has grown from the winds that shaped them.

Being a single parent may not have been your choice. You may wonder whether you or your children will survive this way of life. Being a parent at all in this complicated world of ours is often difficult; being a single parent can be harder still. But it *is* possible to raise responsible, respectful, resourceful children in a single-parent home. And if you're open and willing to learn, you may find that life as a single parent holds opportunities you hadn't thought of, for you *and* for your children.

Wherever you find yourself at this particular moment, you most likely want what most parents want: a family that works for all its members, and children who are growing into capable, contented adults. No, it isn't always going to be easy—but, yes, it *is* possible!

CHAPTER 1

Setting the Stage for Single Parenting

Single parents are, above all else, *parents*. They just happen to be parents who are single. Much of what occupies the minds of single parents is the "single" part: "How much will my children suffer? How will I make enough money to survive? How can I possibly manage when my children are sick and I have to be at work, yet I need to be with them? How will I deal with the emotional rollercoaster, veering from anger to guilt to discouragement and depression? Will I ever find another relationship? And if I do, how do I squeeze in time for dating and still give my children quality time? How do I deal with the anger they display when I want to spend time with other people? Will my children be deprived by not having two parents? How can I be both mother and father? I don't have the time or energy to be *one* effective parent, let alone two. How can I possibly compensate for the hardships my children may experience?"

But there's another part of being a single parent, perhaps the most important part: the plain old everyday "parent" part. Single parents are just that—parents. They deal with the same mundane but often bewildering issues that all parents (including married parents) deal with: "How do I get my kids to do their chores? How can I encourage my teenager to talk to me? What do I do about discipline? Will my kids believe in themselves?

How can I enforce the limits I set? Is there any way to make children stop whining? What about sibling rivalry? Homework? Just getting along?"

Do any of these questions sound familiar? All of these concerns are real, and we will deal with every one of them. Here's a good place to begin: It's a myth that children living with single parents are automatically more deprived than children living with two parents. It could even be *more* harmful for children to live with parents who stay together "for the sake of the children." These parents can't really hide their anger, bitterness, resentments, or despair, and their children may never learn anything about loving, healthy relationships.

Many happy, successful people have been raised by divorced parents, widows, or widowers — or even in orphanages. It is not the circumstances of life, but the way we perceive those circumstances that has the greatest impact. Each person decides whether challenges will be stumbling blocks or stepping stones to joy and success. Understanding this does not negate the struggles and concerns of single parents, but it can offer hope and a basis for dealing with those struggles in ways that benefit children rather than harm them.

Begin by giving up the belief that you have to make it up to your child for being a single parent. Don't try be both mother and father; it's not possible, and it's not even wise. One *healthy* parent is enough. Work toward developing a positive attitude about being a single-parent family: "This is the way it is, and we're going to benefit from the way it is."

Children Follow Your Lead

Children usually pick up the attitudes of their parents. (Sometimes they respond by choosing the opposite.) If you're feeling depressed, deprived, guilty, or tragic, chances are your children will feel the same. If you have a "victim" attitude, chances are your children will feel like victims. If you have an optimistic, courageous attitude, your children will most likely be influenced by it and will probably learn from you. The greatest gift we can give our children is to have a hopeful outlook on life no matter what our circumstances — and all circumstances, no matter how difficult, offer opportunities to learn and grow. Try to focus on how you can make the best of your present opportunities.

Parenting for the Future

Think, for just a few minutes, about the moment you first saw each of your children. Remember the wonder, the awe, the sheer power of those first moments, of that precious new life? All too soon you took that baby home, and life somehow became a constant effort to survive each day, each new adjustment, each new phase. The wonder and awe became a faint memory.

When will the baby sleep through the night? Stand up? Walk? We ponder feeding schedules and developmental charts, and earnestly discuss the various approaches to toilet training. The weeks and months begin to rush by. Before we know it, our children are toddlers and we must decide about discipline. Should we spank? What about "time out"? School days arrive, then the teen years. There are so many day-to-day decisions to be made, and often just dealing with each new behavior (or misbehavior) can take all of our time and energy.

Sooner or later, though, the moment arrives when a proud teenager zooms off in the family car with a group of friends, leaving Mom or Dad to sit in a silent home, surrounded by questions. Is she smoking cigarettes? Marijuana? Is he drinking or partying? What about sex? Does she trust me enough to tell me what's going on in her life? Does he believe in himself? Can she make good choices about life? Did I do enough? Too much? Was I a good enough parent?

All parents face these moments and these questions. Single parents often worry more than most; after all, the responsibility seems to rest squarely on just one all-too-fragile set of shoulders.

If you're reading these words when your children are almost grown, be reassured: it's never too late to make changes, to make things better. If your children are still young, you have the opportunity to shape the future for all of you, to parent your children in a way that is thoughtful, loving, and focused on the future.

Perhaps one of the best things you can do is to take a moment right now and ask yourself a very important question. What is it that you really want for your children? When they grow up and set off to lead their adult lives, what qualities do you want them to possess? And are those qualities nurtured by what you're doing now?

You may want your children to have good judgment, to be responsible, self-reliant, kind, honest, thoughtful, coura-geous, moral, hard-working, appreciative — each parent's list will be a little different. What matters is this: What we do today as parents will shape our children's future. If we want our young ones to be responsible, the way we handle the spilled milk, the broken curfew, or the homework left undone must encourage that quality in them.

This thought feels overwhelming to most parents. "How on earth can I do that?" you may wonder. "Especially as a single parent?" The most important tools are those you already pos-sess: your love for your children, and your own inner wisdom and common sense. Your own life and the decisions you make about it will teach your children a great deal (more, sometimes, than you might like). This book is intended to provide you with additional tools and techniques, and perhaps some new ideas.

If you were to decide to drive across the country from your home to a place you'd never visited before, you'd undoubtedly check a map, plan out the best route, and make sure your car was in good running order. Raising your children should be an equally careful journey. Spending the time now to set your goals as a parent and to think about the long-range results of your actions, will save you untold trouble and confusion farther down the road. As a single parent, with all the distractions and responsibilities that involves, you may find it even more important to have a plan and to know what you want the end result to be. There will undoubtedly be wrong turns and dead ends along the way — there are for all parents.

Taking the time to think about what we want our children to learn from life — and from us — is a critical first step on the road to successful single parenting.

See the Benefits

It may come as a surprise to some that single parenting *can* be successful. As we've already seen, there are benefits to being a single parent. There's a well-perpetuated myth that parenting is always easier when two people share the job. Not necessarily true! It's easy to idealize the advantages of having a partner when you're going it alone, but disharmony often prevails in two-parent households. Mom and Dad hardly ever agree on how parenting should be done. As Alfred Adler put it, "Opposites attract, but they usually have difficulty living together." It's amazing how quickly differences that once seemed endearing become faults that are annoying. Couples who have opposite parenting styles are unlikely to discover this little fact until *after* children arrive.

Look around you and see how many couples disagree as to the "right" kind of parenting — and how often they do battle over the children. One believes in strict control; the other believes in leniency. Their beliefs become even stronger and more pronounced as each feels the need to compensate for the other's misguided ideas. The strict parent becomes stricter to make up for the wishy-washy parent. The lenient parent becomes more lenient to make up for the mean, rigid parent. They argue furiously over who is "right" when they're both being ineffective. In fact, children respond best to something in between, known as *firmness with dignity and respect* — something a single parent can provide quite effectively.

Strict control is ultimately ineffective because it often produces a dangerous combination of rebellion, resentment, revenge, sneakiness, and low self-esteem. Sometimes controlled children become *pleasers* and spend their lives allowing others to control them, often basing their choices in life on the approval and opinion of others. Permissiveness is equally ineffective because it teaches children to manipulate others into giving them whatever they want, without having to put forth any effort on their own. Sometimes children who are raised permissively believe they aren't loved unless someone else is serving them or giving in to them. Either way, the children are not exploring and developing their own capabilities.

By pointing out the problems of dual parenting, we don't mean to imply that children are necessarily harmed if they have two parents. Most single parents occasionally long for a helper, and most married parents occasionally disagree with each other; after all, no situation is perfect. Our purpose is to help single parents stop idealizing dual parenting so they will be more open to other solutions for their problems. Most situations offer both assets and liabilities. You *can* choose to focus on the assets of single parenting.

Assets of Single Parenting

Many people have looked back on their lives and said, "I was so devastated by my divorce that I would never have believed that some day I'd say it was the best thing that ever happened to me — but I'm saying it now. (Well, maybe not the best thing, but a good thing.) I had no idea how much I would grow and improve. I never thought I'd find a relationship that was ten times better than the one I lost. When I became stronger and more mature I was ready for a spouse who was stronger and more mature. I thought my divorce was the end of the world. Actually it was the beginning of a much better world."

When we're immature and insecure, we often (unconsciously) look for mates who have characteristics we lack, as a way of completing ourselves. But soon after we marry these people, instead of feeling complete, we begin a campaign to change our mates—to make them more like us. This does not create a loving, respectful relationship. When we become more mature and secure, we want mates who are similar to us so we can share our interests and lifestyles. When our needs for a shared lifestyle are met, creating a loving, respectful relationship becomes much easier.

Divorce can be extremely painful, especially when it's beyond your control. If you were abandoned, you may be dealing with feelings of rejection, doubts about self-worth, and fear that no one will ever love you again. We strongly suggest that you get into some kind of counseling program to deal with these issues. You can find many free groups through your church or community organizations. Twelve-step programs are usually extremely helpful. Alanon (even if alcohol was not a problem in your life or your relationship) can help you deal with your codependency issues so you can get on with your life.

Essentially you have two choices. You can live the rest of your life with anger, resentment, low self-esteem, or whatever debilitating beliefs run your life, or you can look for the opportunities to learn and grow from whatever circumstances you're faced with. For yourself, and for the sake of your children, we strongly encourage you to use these opportunities to model some of the characteristics you hope your children will develop —courage, tenacity, and confidence in your ability to learn and grow. Many single parents are scared to death of loneliness. They forget that they were often extremely lonely while they were married. They were usually so busy dealing with the distractions of a bad relationship that they didn't take time to feel their loneliness. When the distractions are gone, they have a chance to experience their loneliness and learn from it. There is often much to learn by sitting quietly and meditating on whatever is bothering you. Ask your loneliness, "What do you have to teach me?" You may be surprised at the answers you receive.

We usually don't feel lonely when we have something exciting to do and/or to look forward to. Spend some time making lists of things you have always .wanted to do. (See Chapter 9.)

Shared Responsibility and Contribution

Another asset of single parenting is that children have the opportunity to feel needed (without feeling burdened).

Being a single parent provides an extra incentive to enlist children in shared responsibility. When parents do too much for children, to "make up" for the fact that they have only one parent, the children don't have a chance to develop responsibility, initiative, and new skills. Children who have too many material benefits never learn the strength of character that can come from hard work and delayed gratification. Rather than worrying about the deprivation your children may suffer because you are single, concentrate on giving them a positive outlook and important life skills.

Children develop into capable people when they experience the pride and joy of making a contribution. Participating in shared responsibility—being part of a team—is one way they can gain this experience.

Shared Decision Making

A great way to get children involved in making a contribution is to invite them to share in the decision making through family meetings. (Single-parent families are still families, you know!) Children feel especially capable when they're genuinely needed and when they feel a sense of purpose and significance. In addition to being an excellent way to solve typical problems such as hassles over chores, family meetings allow children to feel needed. Children are much more likely to be enthusiastic and motivated to follow decisions they have helped to make. Let your children help you decide on bedtime routines, morning routines, chore routines, homework routines, planning family-fun events, and anything else it takes to help your family run smoothly. (We will discuss family meetings in more detail in Chapter 8.)

Developing Closeness

The movie *Kramer vs. Kramer* is an excellent illustration of how a father can develop a close relationship with his son as a result of becoming a single parent. The father (Dustin Hoffman) would have missed this wonderful opportunity if he had stayed on his hard-driving career track, leaving all the parenting responsibilities to the mother (Meryl Streep).

With a single parent, kids have a greater opportunity to make meaningful contributions, to feel needed, listened to, and taken seriously, and to develop family closeness. By emphasizing these benefits, we don't mean to say that problems don't exist. But we do mean that idealizing the "greener grass" and maintaining a negative attitude will not help. Focusing on benefits is not the same as ignoring the painful issues and feelings you or your children experience. However, it does help you and your children work through issues and feelings in beneficial ways, as we'll show in the following chapters.

Life presents all kinds of circumstances, some of which we don't like. We can learn, grow, and benefit from life's challenges. We can't control everything that happens, but we can control the ways we *deal* with what happens. As a single parent, you have the opportunity to teach your children this valuable principle. If you've been choosing a negative approach to your situation, acknowledge this to your children and ask for their help. It's never too late to start over.

A Few Points to Keep in Mind

Parenting, especially on your own, is rarely simple. No matter how good the advice you receive, nothing works all the time on all children — or on all parents! Reading a parenting book is a risky business. It's tempting to think "I've done it all wrong," and give up before you start — or to think "This sounds great!" and try to change everything at once. The ideas in this book can be extremely helpful: for instance, many parents, single and married, are raising their children using firmness with dignity and respect. Keeping the following ideas in mind as you read may help you to make the most of what you learn.

1. It is always the relationship that matters most. Tips and techniques are great, but what matters most is a relationship between parent and child that is based on unconditional love and trust. If that relationship is strong — if your children *know* beyond a shadow of a doubt that you love them *no matter what* — you can make a lot of mistakes and still come out okay.

   All parenting skills and ideas work best when they're based on a foundation of love. Techniques without love are just that: techniques. Taking the time to build the proper foundation through words and actions, by talking, laughing, playing, and just being together, may be the best investment you make in your children.

2. Don't try to change everything all at once. You may find as you read that there are many ideas you want to try. But changing too much at once, especially in a single-parent family that may have experienced a great deal of change already, may complicate life instead of making it easier.

   Pick an idea or two at a time and try them for a while. See how they feel, and how your family reacts, before trying anything more. Change that is made gradually and thoughtfully may last longer and be more effective than sudden changes that disrupt the family — and are quickly abandoned.

3. Trust your own wisdom and common sense. No one knows your children better than you do. Your own inner wisdom will tell you when the time is right to make changes in your family — it's usually better to wait until a change *feels* right. Learning to trust your own judgment and to follow your heart as a parent can take time, and you may have to work at developing the confidence to do it, especially if your faith in yourself has been shaken. As you read and think about the rest of this book, let your love for your children be your guide. It will help you decide what you want for your family, what to do, and when it's right to change.

CHAPTER 2

Coping with Feelings: Yours and Theirs

Shouts of anger, irritated nagging, hysterical sobbing, stony silence — the ways we choose to deal with feelings are often anything but productive. So many things can create strong feelings in us: change (such as divorce or death), stress, relationships, sometimes just life itself. What many parents fail to understand is that our children feel the same emotions we do — and have even fewer resources with which to deal with them. Parents always want to be there to help children fix things, whether it's mending a broken doll or finding the missing piece of a favorite game. When children express their feelings, especially strong feelings, parents sometimes want to fix those too, instead of simply understanding them. We want to protect our children, so we often find it difficult to share our feelings honestly. Or we avoid the entire messy subject. "Don't use that tone of voice with me, young man!" we say, or "There's nothing to be afraid of." And children begin to learn that feelings are dangerous things that can cause all sorts of problems — and shouldn't be discussed.

Feelings are an especially sticky subject for single parents. After all, we're likely to have so many of them! Depending on what your experience has been, you're probably familiar with anxiety, loneliness, guilt, fear, anger, bitterness, confusion, and

17

a host of others. When you're in the grip of some of these strong emotions, it can be extremely difficult to deal with the fact that children often feel the same things—and often express them through their behavior. It can be hard to tell the difference between a child who is simply being cantankerous and one who has suffered a loss, is angry and hurt, and is telling you so in the only way he knows how. For all parents—but for single parents in particular—learning to recognize and deal with children's feelings is a critically important first step in dealing with children's behavior.

The truth is that feelings themselves don't cause problems; certain actions (or a failure to act at all) may cause problems. Feelings have a bad reputation because many people put them in the same category as emotional displays. A temper tantrum is an emotional display. Acting depressed is often an emotional display. A feeling, though, is simply a feeling.

Unfortunately, children learn how to deal with their feelings by watching their parents. And most parents deal with difficult feelings either through emotional displays—by dumping their stronger emotions on the people around them—or by squelching them entirely. Unexpressed feelings don't go away, however—they simply go underground. And often when they're finally released, the results are far more damaging than they would have been earlier on.

Feelings give us valuable information. In fact, some of them, like fear, are intended to help keep us safe, to help us sort out foolish actions from wise ones. Other feelings serve as barometers to give us information about what is going on in our lives. Both children and adults can feel frightened by a new experience or a sudden change; they can be justifiably angry when something alters or threatens their world; and they can feel sadness, hurt, and depression. When we are able to tune in to our feelings without judgment or censorship, we can then tune in to our inner wisdom for solutions to the problems that cause these feelings.

It's important to help kids deal with their feelings, such as their disappointment about having only one parent, or their anger if there has been a divorce. Parents can help children express their feelings in ways that don't involve hurting themselves or others. Children (and adults) need to know that feelings are different from actions. Feelings are always okay—they're never right or wrong. What we *do*, on the other hand, might be appropriate or inappropriate.

Many adults are afraid of acknowledging their feelings because they fear it might imply certain actions. For example, they may be afraid to admit they feel discontentment for fear that this will mean they have to make some changes they aren't ready to make. At an unconscious level, they repress their feelings (even though those feelings may leak out in the form of anger or depression). Then this mistaken pattern of denying feelings is passed on to their children. How many times have you heard this exchange? A child says "I hate my sister!" An adult admonishes, "No, you don't. You know you love your sister." This response may lead to a lifetime of repressed feelings. It would be healthier to say to a child, "I can tell how angry or hurt you feel right now. I can't let you hit your sister, but you certainly have a right to express your feelings."

One of the trickiest emotions to handle—and the one considered least tolerable by our society—is anger. Anger is often a way we attempt to take care of ourselves when we're feeling powerless or hurt. Sometimes children display anger because they're frustrated by the controlling demands of their parents. It's one way children (and teenagers!) try to "individuate"—to find out who they are instead of who their parents want them to be.

Children express their angry feelings in all sorts of inappropriate ways—ways that often get them into trouble. Anger, properly expressed, can be a great way to clear the air and set the stage for a discussion of something troubling. Too often, though, anger rages out of control, closing the door on communication and sometimes even putting those we love at risk.

Dealing with Angry Feelings in Appropriate Ways

Alex was six years old when his father moved out, and Diane worried about the effect the breakup of the family would have on her son. Alex was a bright, sensitive boy who was almost always helpful and cheerful. He had never been an aggressive child, so Diane was shocked and confused when one night, during a bedtime tickling match, Alex suddenly began punching her in the stomach.

Diane and Alex had talked quite openly about his father's decision to divorce Diane, but obviously there were feelings in the little boy's heart that even he had no idea were there. The next day, as she drove her son home from school, Diane asked him how he was feeling about what had happened the night before.

Alex was silent for a moment. "Mom," he finally said, "sometimes I feel so angry about stuff that I just want to punch someone!"

Diane was no expert on psychology, but her common sense and her love for her son told her that she had to help him work through these overpowering emotions. "Alex," she said, "you know that you can't hit me when you feel this way. We don't treat each other like that. But I understand how you're feeling, and I think we need to find a way for you to be angry without hurting anyone else."

Diane paid a visit to the toy store and came home with an inflatable "bop bag." Then she told Alex that whenever he was feeling angry or hurt, he could punch the bag. Diane put it in the kitchen so she could talk with Alex when he used it.

Alex and his mother were both surprised at the violence with which he attacked the bag, but with the passage of time, the bop-bag sessions became a source of healing for both of them. Occasionally Diane and Alex would punch the bag back and forth to each other. "Are you angry with Dad too?" Alex asked one day. "You can pretend this is Dad if you want to." More often than not, the punching sessions ended with laughter and hugs.

Alex punched his way through three bop bags before the fourth one died of a slow leak in the kitchen corner. He learned that while his feelings were sometimes difficult to cope with, they were valid and they were *his*, and they were manageable with a little understanding and help. He also discovered that it was possible to be angry with his dad and to still love him very much. That discovery laid the foundation for strong, healthy relationships between Alex and both of his parents.

Diane didn't ignore Alex's feelings, nor did she try to talk him out of them. She didn't plummet into depression, despair, or blame. She helped Alex find a way to work through his feelings in ways that didn't hurt himself or others. The method she chose helped Alex express his feelings of anger until they were manageable and he could focus on other things.

Dealing with your children's strong emotions can be a great opportunity to get into your child's world and to build closeness, understanding, and trust. Here are just a few examples:

1. Ask your child to draw a picture of how the emotion feels. Does it have a color? A sound?

2. Ask your child to talk through what he or she is feeling rather than acting it out.

3. Redirect the behavior in a more appropriate way, as Diane did with Alex.

4. Ask your child to take a cooling-off "time out" period before acting on his or her strong feelings.

It is valuable for both you and your children when you can learn to explore their feelings by getting into their world and seeing things from their perspective. Children living in single-parent homes can experience a wide spectrum of emotions, particularly if they've had to cope with death, or with the divorce of parents, or simply with being different from their friends. They can feel anger, guilt, confusion, worry, sadness, and even fear.

Acknowledging Children's Feelings

"My kids began having bad dreams and difficulty sleeping after their father moved out," one mother reported. "It turned out that they were afraid of burglars now that there was no man in the house. I'd never even thought of that."

Many times the everyday tensions and conflicts we experience with our children result from their feelings. Learning to understand those feelings from a child's perspective — instead of from our own — can help us solve problems rather than exacerbate them. Sometimes, in fact, understanding and accepting feelings are all that's needed to solve a problem. Like us, children need to feel understood and accepted, and careful listening can be a first step to constructive communication.

Heather was planning to go to her father's house for ten days during the Christmas holidays. Although Heather went to her dad's house every other weekend, this visit was to be different. Her grandmother and her aunt were coming from out of town to spend the Christmas holiday with Heather and her father. It had been planned for months. Heather was very excited about seeing her grandmother and meeting her aunt for the first time, but she was used to spending her time with Dad alone. They had wonderful weekends together, in-line skating, taking walks, and playing games. Heather treasured her special time with her father.

On the second day of her visit, Heather called her mother, Christie, in tears because Dad had told her to put on a fancy dress to attend the *Nutcracker Ballet*. "I don't want to wear that dress," Heather wailed. "I want to wear the sweatshirt you gave me."

Christie was in a hurry when her daughter called. "Wear the dress your dad wants," she told Heather briskly. "Santa will probably be at the ballet, and if you're not being good, he'll know."

When Christie hung up the phone, she realized that using Santa Claus to manipulate Heather wasn't fair, nor was it a solution to the problem. Shame and guilt are not good motivators; they don't empower children to make better choices about their behavior. Christie looked forward to an opportunity to be kinder and more respectful the next time she spoke with Heather. Her opportunity came the next day, when Heather called again.

"Dad just made me leave the kitchen. He said I was in the way," she sniffed.

Christie tried to get into Heather's world and to understand the feelings behind the child's behavior. "It sounds like you're feeling left out. Is it hard to share your dad with your grandmother and aunt?"

Heather muttered a sullen "Yeah." She was used to having her dad all to herself, and now he wasn't spending any time with her. "He hasn't played with me at all since I got here, and I'm not having any fun," she said sadly.

Christie asked Heather if she'd thought about telling her dad what she was feeling. Heather was silent for a moment. "Maybe I'll do that," she said.

When Christie's phone rang the next day, a much happier child was on the other end. "I told Dad what we were talking about, Mom," she said, "and he agreed to play with me at least once each day. And this morning we went for a walk alone — just the two of us." Heather chattered cheerfully with her mother for a few minutes more, then hung up, leaving Christie smiling.

When Heather felt understood, she was then able to approach her problem from a different perspective — and find a solution to it.

Reflective Listening: The Key to Communication

Reflective listening is the art of listening to, and reflecting back, a child's feelings. It gives the parent a chance to explore the feelings behind the child's behavior. Reflective listening does not necessarily mean that the parent is agreeing with the child, but it allows a child to feel understood — something all of us need from time to time — and an opportunity to clarify her own feelings and move on to problem solving.

Ron's 15-year-old son returned home after a visit to his mother with a sour expression on his face. "Hi there, Mark," Ron called out. "I missed you. When you've had a chance to straighten up your room, we can go have that ball game we talked about."

Mark, as it happened, had not had a good weekend. Mom's new boyfriend was visiting — with his two young sons — and Mark had had to share both his room and his possessions with them. He was feeling displaced and angry, and the thought of cleaning his room at home was more than he could bear. "I don't care about playing ball," he told his bewildered father, "and I'm *not* going to clean my room!" He disappeared into his room with a resounding slam of the door, leaving Ron to wonder what he should do next.

Ron had several options. He could open the door and insist that Mark clean his room. He could tell Mark angrily, "Don't talk to me that way!" (Does this sound familiar? Parents often tell their children how to feel or how not to feel, instead of just listening and acknowledging the feeling.)

The option Ron chose was to give Mark a moment to cool off. Then he reflected back Mark's feelings. "Sounds like you're pretty angry," he said gently, when Mark finally opened his bedroom door. Mark grunted noncommittally. "You seem to be feeling hurt, too," his dad continued. "Is there something you'd like to talk about?" It took a moment, but Mark began to tell his father about his weekend with Mom and how he'd felt. Once Mark realized that his dad understood and accepted his feelings, they worked together on finding solutions to the problems, to Mark's behavior towards his dad, and to the issue of cleaning his room. And later there was still time for the ball game.

Parents must learn to be alert to nonverbal clues, too. A normally cheerful child who comes home from school and goes silently to her room may be giving you a clue that she needs to talk. A slammed door, a quivering chin, or an inability to sleep at night may be evidence that your child needs to sort through some feelings with you.

When we learn to reflect back and empathize with the statements — both verbal and nonverbal — made by our children, we give them an opportunity to think about what has happened, a moment to probe for the true feeling. When we contest what they have said, or lecture, or rationalize, we're only challenging them to argue their position or to refuse to talk at all. And we may miss important opportunities for healing, for showing love, and for building trust.

A child may say "No one wants to play with me." A nonreflective response would be "Oh, come on now, you have lots of friends." While the parent's statement may be true, it doesn't acknowledge the child's feeling at that moment — and it effectively closes off any real communication about what's going on.

A reflective response would be "You seem to think you don't have any friends. I can see that makes you sad." When the child has had a chance to respond, a parent might follow up by asking, "Is there more?" This question often brings out deeper, buried feelings. Sometimes all children *really* need is for someone to listen and understand. Thoughtful, reflective listening gives parents the chance to understand — and to deal with what's really important.

Here are a few examples of reflective listening. Pretend these statements are made by a child. How would you respond?

1. No one ever invites me to their party!

2. It hurts when I go to the dentist!

3. I don't like my teacher at school!

4. You're not fair!

Reflective listening might lead you to offer responses like this:

1. Sounds like you're disappointed that you weren't invited to a party. Is there more?

2. It can hurt sometimes when you go to the dentist — sometimes I don't like going either!

3. You sound frustrated with your teacher. Is there something else?

4. Sounds like you think I made a mistake. Can you tell me why you feel that way?

These statements invite children to be heard and to know it's okay to feel what they feel. Validating a child's feelings with love and understanding is a wonderful way to open the door for real communication and to build a relationship of trust.

Dealing With Loss: The Miracle of Time and Patience

One of the hardest things for parents to accept is that we cannot change our children's feelings, or protect them from unpleasant ones. Children feel grief and loss just as acutely as adults do. It's tempting to try to reason our children out of their pain, not because we don't understand but because we don't want them to suffer. Most of the time, however, the most helpful thing a loving parent can do is simply to listen, accept, and be patient.

Jackie had always been careful to plan for emergencies with her children. They knew their phone numbers, who to call, and what to do if Mom was late picking them up from school. So, when a late meeting and several red lights made Jackie about five minutes late one afternoon, she wasn't overly concerned. Seven-year-old Clint knew that he could talk to the school secretary if he was worried, and that he should wait in front of the school for his mom to arrive.

So Jackie was both surprised and alarmed when she pulled up at the school one afternoon to find the principal sitting on a low wall next to a hysterical little boy.

"What's wrong?" she called out, almost tripping in her rush to get out of the car. She knelt down next to Clint, looking anxiously into his tear-stained face. "What happened, honey?"

The principal gave her a gentle, sympathetic smile. "Your little boy was afraid you weren't coming," she said. "He panicked a little."

Clint's sobs subsided into occasional sniffles as they drove home. "Clint," his mom began. "I can see you're really upset, but I don't understand why. You didn't used to be so clingy. We've talked about what you could do if I was late. Why didn't you just wait for me to come?"

There was a long pause; Clint's answer was almost a whisper. "I thought something might have happened to you, Mom," he said. "I thought you weren't coming."

"But honey," Jackie began, "you *know* I would never leave..." And then, with a flash of insight, she understood what her son was feeling. His dad had died unexpectedly only a few months before, and suddenly Jackie understood just how fragile life must seem to her small son. What would happen to him if Mom were gone too?

Jackie pulled the car over at the first safe place and scooped Clint into her arms. "I miss your dad, too, and sometimes I'm just as scared as you are. I guess I can't always control what happens, but I would never *choose* to leave you, Clint. You and your sister are the most important people in my life, and I'll always do my best to be there for you."

The pain and fear her son felt almost broke Jackie's heart. Even harder was the realization that she couldn't make those feelings all better the way she'd cured his "owies" when he was tiny. Children do grieve, whether it's for a parent, for a lost pet, or for a shattered dream. The hope that all parents have, for themselves and for their children, is that time is indeed a healer.

It's normal for children who have suffered the loss of one parent, for whatever reason, to cling to the parent who remains, to cry when that parent leaves, and to worry when he or she is even a little late returning. Though such dependency can be frustrating, the simple rhythm and routine of normal life are soothing. It helps, too, to talk about your schedule with your children, to make contingency plans with them, and to reassure them that you'll do your best to be there when you're expected (and that you'll call if your plans change).

Experts tell us that it can take two or three years to recover from the loss of a loved one. Whether your children have lost a parent to death or divorce, you can't rescue them from the pain. Only time and understanding will ease it. You *can* listen, accept their feelings, and—when appropriate—share your own . And be patient—it may not seem possible, but it will get better.

What About My Own Feelings?

Feelings—sad ones and glad ones—are a part of the human condition. They aren't likely to go away any time soon. Parents are often struggling with their own topsy-turvy emotions: we feel hurt, rejection, worry, stress. And, like our children's, our feelings can influence the way we behave. Parents don't do their best work when they're tired, hurting, or overwhelmed, and sometimes our children bear the brunt of how we feel—without understanding why.

"But I'm furious at my ex-wife," you may think. Or, "I'm feeling so panicky and afraid that I can't function." "Sometimes," you may say, "those kids make me so angry I can't help myself."

How much of their own feelings should parents show? Is it wise to let our children see that we're angry or sad or afraid?

Covering up or denying our feelings rarely works. Those who know us well generally can sense what we're feeling. In fact, children possess incredibly sensitive antennas when it comes to detecting moods and emotions, and without a better explanation they often assume that *they* are the cause of whatever their parents are feeling. Even worse is denying our pain and taking it out on our children — yelling and screaming about a messy kitchen instead of saying, "I'm feeling scared and overwhelmed right now. I need some time to myself until I can feel better."

As tricky as it can be sometimes, it's best to talk honestly about what you're feeling, especially when the family is going through times of change or stress. Not only does a parent's emotional honesty help children understand what's really happening, it encourages them to express their own feelings honestly as well. You can share the simple fact of what you're feeling ("I'm really angry at your dad right now") without including blame or details that children don't need to know.

Parents can even express their feelings of displeasure with their children's behavior in a nonjudgmental way. All too often our "constructive criticisms" of our children are accompanied by a great deal of finger-pointing and an unpleasant tone of voice. It's possible to say simply, "When you don't come home when you've promised to, I feel scared and upset because I love you and I worry that something has happened to you. I'd appreciate it if you would phone me when you're going to be late." Children are far more likely to understand the true situation — and parents are far less likely to lose control — when feelings can be expressed honestly but with respect.

Laura, a single mother, had just arrived home after a long day at work. She was late getting dinner together, and she was exhausted; in addition, she had an early meeting the next day and still needed time alone that evening to prepare for it. She longed for peace and quiet—and her two daughters were arguing about who would get to use the bathroom first. As the argument gathered steam, they clamored for Laura to decide who was right. Laura felt her own tension level begin to rise. Finally she could take no more, and she began to yell too, lecturing the girls about getting along. When she paused for breath, she realized that what was happening was more her problem than the children's. She was too tired to respond rationally to their sibling rivalry.

Laura turned to the children with emotional honesty. She said quietly, "Girls, I'm too tired tonight to have the patience for your arguing." She explained that she'd had a long day, would have another the next day, and needed to take care of herself. She asked the girls to please work their problem out between themselves and then put themselves to bed. Then she said goodnight, gave them each a hug, and went off to her room.

Because Laura rarely needed to ask for this kind of time alone, and because she had shared her feelings with sincerity instead of lecturing and blaming, her daughters were able to allow her the time alone—and to work out their dispute over the bathroom on their own.

We often overreact with frustration, disappointment, or an irrational form of discipline when we're feeling low or tired. What we really need is to take care of ourselves by letting our children know how we're feeling, helping them understand what's going on in our world, and teaching them to be supportive. Children should never be asked to carry burdens too heavy for them or to take the place of a missing adult, but simple explanations of how we're feeling can make all the difference between a storm of anger, guilt, and blaming, and a loving and cooperative atmosphere.

Going Too Far: What If I Lose Control?

Learning to deal with our emotions honestly and constructively can do more than keep our homes peaceful—it can save those we love from injury and fear. No parent intends to hurt a child, but the sad reality is that stress, frustration, and anger can lead us to behave in ways we later regret, or to use drugs or alcohol to ease the tension.

Picking up his sons, Billy and Eric, at the day care center was the high point of Joe's day. Joe, a single dad, worked hard and was often tired, but he loved to scoop the boys up for a hug, inspect their artwork, and talk about how their day had gone. When they arrived home, Joe would prepare dinner and unwind a bit—with a few drinks. And the more Joe "unwound," the more annoyed he became with Billy's and Eric's behavior.

One evening after dinner, Joe slumped in his chair, watching as his sons tried to help clear the table. There were bills to be paid—too many bills—and the car wasn't running properly. Joe had had an argument with the boys' mother about visitation, and his anger led him to unwind just a bit more than usual. Just as Joe finished a drink, Billy dropped a casserole dish—and Joe exploded. He dragged the crying child into his room where he lectured him about his clumsiness. "I need some fresh air," he thought. He locked the door to Billy's room, told Eric to watch TV, and headed out—to the neighborhood bar.

Several hours later, the police stopped Joe and cited him for driving under the influence of alcohol. When the boys were discovered home alone, child abuse and neglect were added to the charge. It took the intervention of the legal system, but Joe was able to get weekly counseling to deal with his drinking. He also attended a parenting class to learn some new skills.

Despite his unquestioned love for his sons, Joe went too far. So do many parents who resort to physical punishment, or to emotional and verbal abuse. How does a stressed-out parent, particularly a single parent who may be raising children alone under difficult circumstances, stay in control?

It helps to have a support network (see Chapter 4), a circle of friends who can offer an attentive ear. And it's vital to learn to recognize your own danger signals: a tense jaw, clenched fists, a pounding heart, or a rising voice may tell you it's time to be careful. Drugs and alcohol are never constructive solutions to any problem.

Do We Control Our Feelings? Or Do They Control Us?

It's tempting to let our feelings control us or to use them as excuses for our less-than-wonderful actions. When we are able to listen to our feelings, to accept and learn from them, however, we can act thoughtfully and make the best choices in even difficult situations.

Andrea had been out of town for the weekend at a workshop and she was looking forward to picking up her eight-year-old daughter, Amy, at her father's house. Amy usually missed her mother when they were separated and Andrea hummed cheerfully to herself as she drove, looking forward to a big hug. She took Amy out for pizza. When they got home they took a walk after unpacking, talking about what they had done while they were apart, and then curled up to read together before Amy went to bed.

Andrea was sitting at the kitchen table sorting through the weekend mail when she saw her daughter trailing hesitantly down the hall towards her. "What's up, honey?" she asked. "Can't you sleep?"

"I'm going to call my dad," Amy responded. Andrea waited quietly, trying not to glance impatiently at the clock. It was a short conversation; Andrea could tell that John, her ex-husband, was busy with something. Amy slowly hung up the phone and when she turned to face her mother there were tears trickling down her cheeks.

Andrea reached out for her daughter. "You look awfully sad, pumpkin," she said. "Do you want to tell me what's wrong?"

Amy hesitated, and Andrea could see that she was reluctant to speak. Finally, out it came. "I can't sleep because I miss my dad, Mom. We had *such* a good time this weekend and I just want to be with him right now."

Andrea felt stung. It had been more than three years since she and John had divorced. The adjustment had been terribly difficult, but Andrea had been determined to do what was best for her daughter, even helping her maintain her relationship with her father when Amy had been hurt and disillusioned in him. It had been a painful process, but in the past months the emotional trauma and upheaval had subsided. She had begun to feel secure and optimistic about both her own life and her daughter's. John was going to remarry soon and Amy was thrilled with all of the wedding plans; Andrea had even managed to cope with that. But now here was Amy, obviously still caught in the middle.

"Well, what do you want to do, Amy? What would make you feel better?" Andrea asked.

Amy's answer was immediate. "I want to go back to my dad's house. I want to sleep there and then he can take me to school in the morning."

Andrea's face must have mirrored her hurt. "But honey, I just got home," she said. "Don't you want to be with me?" She watched her daughter struggle, suddenly aware that Amy was caught between her own needs and the desire to avoid hurting her mother. Pleasing her mother won.

"Oh, never mind, Mom," Amy suddenly said. "I'll be okay. I'll just go back to bed." She turned to go to her room, but not before her mother saw her trembling chin.

Andrea took a deep breath. "Amy," she said, "I'm not sure what your dad will say, but we can call him and ask if he's willing to come to pick you up. Is that what you really want?"

"Oh yes," Amy replied, and ran for the phone. This time the conversation was longer and when Amy hung up she was smiling. "He's going to come right away, Mom," she said, and ran off to pack some clothes for the morning.

When John arrived, he had a sympathetic smile for Andrea. "Are you sure you're okay with this?" he asked. "I don't want to interfere with your time with Amy."

"Well," Andrea replied as Amy came down the hall, "it's what she seems to need right now. Yeah, it hurts a little, but I'll be okay."

Andrea managed a smile and hug for her daughter and then closed the door behind her. "Oh well," she told herself as she walked back to the kitchen table. "It doesn't really matter. I'm really glad she's able to tell me what she wants . . . " Andrea's thoughts trailed off and suddenly she was crying.

"It *hurts*," she thought, sitting down in a heap on the couch as the reality of how she felt hit her. "How can it still hurt so much?"

Amy called the next morning. "I'm sorry, Mom," she said softly. "I guess sometimes I want both you *and* Dad, and I don't know what to do."

Andrea was able to respond with a smile in her voice. "Amy, it took courage to tell me what you felt. I'm glad you did." They chatted for a few minutes before Amy, reassured, went off to school.

"I still feel so insecure and afraid sometimes," Andrea told her best friend later that day. "I guess I still think I'm going to lose her. I *hate* sharing my daughter, even with her own father. I think I did the right thing, but Amy's wanting to leave me really hurt. I feel like I've had a knot in my chest ever since last night."

Her friend smiled at her sympathetically. "You did what you thought was best for Amy. That takes courage. And Amy learned that she can trust you with her feelings. Have faith, Andrea, in your daughter and in your relationship with her. You'll both be just fine."

It may not always be necessary (or even wise) to go along with what our children want. Sometimes we may be encouraging our children to be manipulative when we jump in and try to fix every emotional upset. In this case, however, Andrea trusted her instincts that Amy was struggling with an emotional conflict that involved a genuine need to work things out in her own way. Even though it hurt, Andrea was willing to listen and accept her daughter's feelings, trusting that this would eventually lead to a greater degree of closeness between them.

Unfortunately, as Andrea learned, doing the right thing doesn't always feel good. Sometimes choosing what is best for our children can be difficult, even painful. It is still possible to act in *spite* of our feelings rather than allowing ourselves to be controlled by them.

When Amy came home the next afternoon she gave her mother an extra-big hug before she went out to play. And there was an opportunity later in the evening for Andrea to talk with Amy and to explain a little of how she had felt. Both mother and daughter learned that it was okay to be honest with each other and that difficult situations, handled without anger or blaming, can be opportunities to build trust and closeness.

Remember, even the most difficult feelings are still just feelings. But the way we deal with them can be either constructive or destructive to us and to those we love. When anger and stress become overwhelming, both children and adults can learn to take "time out"— not as a punishing confinement, but as a way to cool off and feel better so that a situation can be discussed calmly. We can find alternate ways of expressing frustration: yelling into a pillow, rather than at a person, can work wonders. Even children can learn to count to ten, to take deep breaths, and to discuss problems calmly. One dad reported that when anger threatened to take over, he took out the garbage and dumped it forcefully and noisily into the can. By the time he returned to the house he was in control and ready to find constructive solutions to the problems on his mind.

Changing the way we handle our stronger emotions takes time and energy, and we won't always be successful. But teaching our children — and ourselves — to deal positively with feelings allows us to be real, and saves all that energy we spend suppressing or venting our emotions for far better uses. Taking the time to practice reflective listening, to understand the way our children are feeling, and to help them understand us is also a wonderful and highly practical way to build a relationship of trust and understanding, which will carry us through years of growing, changing, and difficult times.

CHAPTER 3

Balancing, Juggling, and Other Single-Parenting Skills

It had been a frustrating day at work, and Lynne felt tired and cranky as she flopped down on the couch to figure out what she could accomplish before the end of the day.

A pile of bills waited on the desk, the carpet was speckled with pebbles from the shoes of three children who had obviously had a fine time in the school sandbox, and the kitchen floor was spattered with sticky spots where some Kool-Aid had missed its target. Come to think of it, Lynne mused, the bathrooms probably needed cleaning too. And the car needed an oil change.

Lynne's mind began to whirl. It was almost time for dinner. Was there anything in the refrigerator? She gazed wearily out into the yard, but that only reminded her that the lawn needed watering, fertilizing, and mowing—in who knew what order? And at that moment, Lynne's children plopped down by her side with a stack of books. "Can you read to us, Mom?" they asked.

It was a moment of revelation. The sea of emotions calmed, the dust settled, the mist cleared, and the sunlight revealed the handwriting on the wall. "Welcome," it said, "to the land of single parenting. Watch your step."

It doesn't matter whether you're divorced or widowed, male or female, custodial or noncustodial. Being a single parent can be one of life's trickiest balancing acts. There's too much to be done and, all too often, too little time in which to do it.

In a "traditional" home, a couple shares in some fashion the tasks of running a household and caring for children. In a single-parent home, those same tasks remain, but suddenly there is only one pair of adult hands to do the work, and the prospect can seem overwhelming.

Single parents often report that it's the little things that send them over the edge. There's now no one to watch the kids for a minute while you take a quick shower or run to the store; no one else to catch the mutilated but still living mouse the cat has brought in; no one to help mend a torn garment, explain why the car won't start, do the laundry, mow the lawn, or shovel the snow.

Worst of all, there's no one to talk to at the end of the day when the children are asleep, no one to share concerns and small triumphs with. The traditional partner in raising children, the other parent, may be completely out of the picture or completely unsympathetic. Single parents frequently complain of feeling isolated, and no wonder! There's never enough time to get everything done. The result is often a complicated and over-whelming combination of frustration, guilt, worry, and exhaustion—not exactly an atmosphere that encourages the kind of relationships we want to have with our children.

How, then, do you cope? When the grieving and adjusting have been done and life has settled into a semblance of normalcy —however stressful—what then?

How does a single parent balance all of the demands on his or her time, raise children effectively, and still find time to learn, to grow, and to enjoy life? Is it even possible? We will show you that it *is* possible.

Sorting Our Priorities: What's Most Important, Anyway?

It used to be said that children of single parents came from "broken" homes, but it's vital to realize that your home isn't broken unless you let it be. Single-parent families can function just as effectively and efficiently as the two-parent variety, nurturing and encouraging children who grow up to be capable, healthy adults. But there's no doubt that it takes some thought, some planning, and, occasionally, a little extra help.

Time, as they say, is money. Yet we frequently budget our dollars carefully while we spend our time without thought or plan, wondering at the end of a frantic day why we got so little accomplished. Thoughtfully sorting out priorities may be one of the most effective things any parent, but especially a single parent, can do.

There are some things in life we can't avoid—work or school, for instance—but we make a statement about what things are important in our lives by deciding how much discretionary time we spend on them. Some of those choices can be difficult: do we concentrate on work and career, or do we make time with children a priority? Do we hop onto the fast track, hoping for advancement and the benefits that it might bring to our family? Or do we spend less time at work, settling for fewer financial rewards, perhaps, but being more involved in our children's daily lives? What are the long-range results of each decision, for us and for our children? Answers to such fundamental questions will be different for each parent and will require a great deal of thought. However, deciding where the time goes day by day can be a bit easier to manage. It can be immensely helpful to keep track, for a week or so, of exactly how much time we actually spend on each activity in our lives. The results are often surprising. That done, it's fairly simple to look at the available time in our week and decide what's *really* most important and how much time we want to spend on each activity.

It may be helpful to budget time during each week for family activities. If we don't plan them, sometimes they don't happen at all. Looking at the way we approach our unavoidable chores can be helpful: a little advance planning may make one weekly trip to the grocery store possible, for example, instead of daily ones.

There are any number of creative ways to readjust priorities and responsibilities so that they fit better into a limited amount of time. Here are just a few suggestions for reorganizing time and effort:

1. **Eliminate unrealistic expectations.** Your mother may have kept her floors spotless, ironed her pillowcases, and placed elegantly prepared meals on the dining room table each evening precisely at 6:30, but that doesn't mean you have to—or even should. Look at what's possible, and keep your expectations of yourself realistic. It will take time and some experimentation, but learn to be content with what you can do effectively.

2. **Try making lists.** Prioritize each day's tasks on paper, and do the most important ones first. Not only will lists help you get things done, but crossing items off can be one of the most satisfying parts of your day! Try to do small tasks (such as paying a bill or sewing on a loose button) as they come up, rather than piling them up for later.

3. **Cooking.** Getting dinner on the table after a day of work can be a single parent's nightmare. Try preparing dishes (when you do have the time) that will provide good leftovers, such as a casserole or a roast turkey. Or prepare double portions on weekends and put what's left into the freezer for a busy day. Get older children involved in planning and preparing meals—it can be a great learning experience for all of you!

3. **Housecleaning.** This is one part of family life that seems to get out of hand for all single parents. Cleaning can be more fun when everyone in the family works together. It's surprising how much can get done when everyone pitches in for 10 minutes a day or two hours once a week. Try doing a little bit every day, rather than a lot all at once. Provide each member of the family with baskets for laundry—even young children can learn to put white clothes in one basket and dark ones in another. Tackle cleaning one room each day. Make some family rules on picking up toys and clothes, and enforce the rules you set. (More on that later.)

4. **Take time to teach.** It may not seem so at the time, but teaching children how to help out with domestic duties can save you time later on—as well as giving your children the basic skills to make their own way in life. Work alongside them, showing them how a job can best be done; next, supervise in a friendly way as they do it alone. Before long, they'll be able to do the work to your satisfaction without your involvement. Just be careful not to set your standards too high!

5. **Don't forget to make time for fun.** Housework and chores seem a lot easier to bear when a good time is waiting at the end. You may choose to have the entire family do house and yard work on Saturday morning, saving the rest of the day for an activity you have planned together. Be sure to leave time in your week for togetherness and fun—those are the times that will make you *feel* like a family.

Some things may need to be moved far down your list of priorities. Given the choice between an evening cuddle with a child who needs to talk and scouring the bathroom, it may be wise to choose the cuddle. The house may not be as spotless as you'd like, but housework will wait; missed moments with children may never come again.

Don't Let Your Children Get Lost in the Shuffle

Helping our children develop their full potential is a top priority for all caring parents, and one that can be all too easily neglected when the hassles of daily life intrude.

Have you ever stood outside the door of a young child and listened?

"Pretend your guy is riding up on his horse," one child will say. "Yeah, and then pretend that my guy is in the castle," another chimes in. "And then there's an *earthquake!*" another shouts, and the room echoes with the sounds of falling Legos and laughter.

Imagination and creativity are wonderful gifts. Creative children believe in all sorts of possibilities and are also able to believe in themselves and in their ability to tackle and solve a problem. Experts also tell us, however, that creative, thoughtful children are the ones who ask those steady streams of irritating questions. They love to invent new rules for games and new ways of doing things — often to the annoyance of their harassed parents.

Unfortunately, it's often the most creative children who are labeled "troublemakers" because they ask too many questions and because they seem to find it impossible to be still and do exactly what everyone else is doing. Perhaps every child has the potential to be creative — but because creative, energetic children can complicate life for busy teachers and parents, they're often taught early to squelch their enthusiasm and to conform with the crowd. We may never know what talents and ideas have been lost in exactly this way.

Our lives as busy single parents leave little time for the special and out-of-the-ordinary. It is difficult enough to listen to everything our children say and to deal with the endless crises of daily life. Encouraging specialness takes time and energy that we may not feel we have.

Creative children are not always those who play the violin at three, or the piano at five, or who read or paint or study ancient history at an early age. What about the child whose gifts are less obvious? What about the child who simply has a knack for solving a problem? Or who has a vivid imagination and a talent for storytelling? Or a deep and genuine love for ideas?

We need to learn to recognize and to encourage the uniqueness of our children. It helps to turn off the television and read or talk about what our children find interesting. Be patient with their questions, their different approaches. Let them try something new occasionally or experiment with a new idea. Ask yourself whether they're challenging the status quo just to be contrary, or because they really do have a better idea.

Above all, let them know you love and value them for exactly who they are, differences and special qualities included. The pressure to go along with the majority is overwhelming enough as it is. It takes patience and perseverance, but teaching our children to value their own uniqueness just may be the thing that sets them off on the road to a creative and productive life.

Keeping Things in Perspective

Maintaining our perspective on what is most important can take some of the frustration out of balancing priorities. Lisa is a single mother whose three-year-old daughter, Abby, always seemed to come home from preschool dirty—so dirty that cleaning her up and doing the laundry each night had become a constant irritation to Lisa.

"It's more than I can handle," Lisa complained to a group of single parents. "This afternoon when I picked Abby up, she was soaking wet from playing in a stopped-up water fountain, and she was muddy, too." Lisa heaved a sigh. "My days are hectic enough without this. I'm angry at Abby, and I'm angry at the preschool."

The group understood what Lisa was saying: staying abreast of a busy life can leave single parents without the energy to handle unexpected mishaps with grace and patience. But they suggested to Lisa that active three-year-olds are bound to get dirty. The group also encouraged Lisa to do something about her suspicion that the preschool might be lax in their organization and supervision of the children. A father who had experienced a similar situation suggested that visiting the preschool and observing for a while might help Lisa decide what, if anything, could be done to change the situation. Spending time to observe might seem time-consuming now, he said, but it could eventually save Lisa a lot of the time she now spent worrying and fretting about her dirty daughter, and it might put her mind at rest about the quality of care Abby was receiving. Realizing that other parents faced similar problems and thinking through some solutions helped Lisa regain her perspective.

It's easier to maintain a healthy outlook when you have interests in life besides your children. Regardless of how busy you may be, one of your priorities should be *you*. It won't just happen: you have to make time to nurture yourself. You can't answer every demand made on you, no matter how hard you try, and you'll have nothing to give if you allow yourself to become empty. Recognize your limitations. Learn to say "no" on occasion. You and everyone around you will benefit if you take time to do something you enjoy, whatever it might be, on a regular basis. Read a book, take a hot bath, listen to music, tinker with machinery, spend time with friends. (Yes, your children can survive without you once in a while!) You can model self-esteem for your children by being good to yourself. Your children will learn that taking care of oneself is important, and they will learn to respect others' needs. And you'll find yourself becoming a healthier, calmer parent—and a happier human being.

What About Leaving My Children?

For many single parents, leaving their children, whether it's to go to work or to take some time for themselves, is a real problem. We yearn to get away; then, once we're gone, we worry ourselves silly. Child care is expensive and can be difficult to find. You may be lucky enough to have a trustworthy teenager nearby, or you may be able to share child care with neighbors or form a babysitting co-op. There's one option that, however tempting it may seem to harried single parents, must be considered very carefully before you try it: leaving children home alone.

Unfortunately, not all children are as resourceful as the young hero of the popular movie. Leaving children home alone may be convenient for parents, and sometimes it may seem to be the only option available, but it can be an invitation to disaster for children. Is it ever okay to leave children on their own? If so, when?

Judging when a child can handle staying alone depends on many things, and age isn't always the best way to tell. It goes without saying that very young children should never be left unattended, but some younger children can handle being alone while older ones cannot.

If you have *any* doubts, don't leave a child alone, and never leave for longer than an hour or so. But if you believe that your child is mature enough to understand the situation and the rules involved in keeping him or herself safe, it may be fine — provided that you structure the situation carefully.

Be sure your child feels comfortable with being alone. Branches scratching the window, or a cat yowling outside, can be terrifying to a child alone in a silent house. Of course, the situation can become a lot more volatile when more than one child is involved. Unless you've got a teen or a responsible pre-teen to rely on, never leave children in charge of their younger siblings. The responsibility is just too great, and too many things can go wrong.

If you're confident that your child can handle being alone for a short time, there are some steps you should take to make the situation as safe as possible:

1. Talk with your child about what might happen while you're gone. Leave a key for doors that may be bolted. Outline a way out of the house in case of fire or emergency. Write down emergency numbers and be sure your child understands how to use them. The number of a friend or neighbor who's home may be helpful as well.

2. Discuss with your child what to do if someone comes to the door or calls for a parent who isn't home. You may want to make some rules about who may or may not be in the house while you're away.

3. Set some guidelines for activities that are allowed. For instance, watching television, playing video games, and playing quietly are fine, but cooking or experimenting with the chemistry set may not be appropriate without adult supervision.

4. Never simply ask a child if he understands the rules — he'll always tell you he does. Write down the rules you've agreed upon, post them where they can easily be seen, and have your child repeat them to you to check his understanding. If he isn't comfortable with the rules you've agreed on, don't leave!

Single parents frantically juggling too many responsibilities may be tempted to leave children alone "just for a little while." If the child is responsible and mature, it may be just fine to do so. But before you close the door behind you, think a moment about all that can happen while you're away. Our children are precious and irreplaceable and our convenience is never worth putting them at risk.

Your priorities, the demands on your time, and life itself will change periodically, and you may find that what works one month may need adjustment the next. But investing some time and thought in sorting out all the things you "have to do" will pay off in reduced stress and frustration, and in a more peaceful home.

CHAPTER 4

"Help! I'm Overwhelmed!"

There comes a time in the life of most single parents when it all just seems to be too much to cope with. We find ourselves dreaming about Tahiti or Alaska or some nameless, deserted place where we can be at peace and "they" (whoever "they" are) can't find us. Single parents may be more susceptible than most to these feelings of being overwhelmed and burned out. We feel alone and overburdened, without help or resources. We're all alone up there on the tightrope, and there's no safety net.

But there should be. One of the most important tasks for a single parent is to begin to build that safety net, a support system that will give us resources to rely on when the anxieties and pressures in our lives threaten to engulf us. Learning to deal with all the demands on our time isn't easy, but it's critical to our effectiveness and our peace of mind as single parents.

How Will I Survive? Dealing with Job and Financial Pressure

One of the most overwhelming aspects of single parenthood, especially in the first months, is the feeling of insecurity and anxiety that comes from financial stress. Each single parent has his or her own litany of woe: "I don't make enough money. I don't have any skills except waitressing. My ex-spouse doesn't pay child support—how will I ever make it? My family lets me live with them, but they don't have much money and my children and I are a real drain on them financially and emotionally—to say nothing of the arguments we get into about how to discipline the children. What can I do? And how on *earth* will I ever pay for college?"

What *can* single parents do to ease job and financial pressures?

Sometimes it seems unavoidable to give in to panic. But panic and fear often short-circuit constructive approaches to problem solving. If financial worries are overwhelming, begin solving them by taking the small steps that you *can* handle.

1. Don't be ashamed to ask for help if you need it. Seek help from welfare agencies if you have to, and then make a plan to learn a skill and get off welfare as soon as you can. Many churches and social agencies have food and clothing closets that can provide you with a boost over the difficult places. If your pride gets in your way, promise yourself that one day you'll be in a position to help someone else.

2. You may want to find one or two other single parents in the same boat. Share housing and child care responsibilities. Use family meetings (see Chapter 8) at which all the parents and all the children get together to create routines, solve any problems that arise, and prevent anticipated problems in advance by creating solutions before they're needed.

3. If you don't have an extended family or a spouse who shares time with your children, start a children's play group swap. Find two to four other single parents who are willing to swap kids for one weekend day. If there are four parents, each one takes all the kids for one weekend day a month. That leaves three free weekend

days for each parent. The play groups can be well organized and can include art activities, games, stories, and simple cooking experiences. Even if only two parents are swapping, they each have two free weekend days and two weekend days in which they can enjoy their children more because of thoughtful planning.

4. Self-pity and anger at your ex-spouse can keep you stuck in negative thinking and can make it difficult to take positive steps. It may take time, but work on giving up your "victim" mentality and your anger. Focus your energy on solutions, take time to nurture yourself, and remember that your attitude really does make all the difference.

5. You may want to visit the library and find motivational books or tapes, or inspirational stories of others' successes under similar circumstances. Be open to new ideas and to learning from someone else's experiences.

6. If you don't have an education, get one. Start by taking one class each semester at a low-cost community college or technical college. It took one of the authors 11 years (and five children) to obtain a bachelor of arts degree; she started because someone advised her to take one class at a time. See a counselor about scholarships for low-income students, which may pay tuition and some living expenses while you're in school.

7. Learn to budget your money. We live in an age of affluence and materialism. Some financial problems have less to do with being a single parent than with poor budgeting skills. It's true that you may have to go without a fancy wardrobe and car, nice furniture, and eating out, at least for a while. However, many successful people can tell you stories of strict budgeting and "going without" during their early days.

Too many single parents think their children are deprived if they have to "go without," and it can be tempting to try giving children material things to make up for their loss of a two-parent family. But take a moment to think about the message this attitude is giving children about the importance of *things*. When you adopt a positive attitude about budgeting and the long-range benefits of delayed gratification, you teach your children many skills that will serve them far better than materialism. This could even prove to be an advantage over affluent two-parent families.

Teach your children about budgeting by involving them in the process. During a family meeting, discuss how much money is available for the week. Explain where money comes from and what bills you must pay, and talk about the need to save for unexpected expenses. Let the kids help decide some ways you might save money. Invite them to help you brainstorm free or low-cost ways to have fun, such as family game nights, trips to the park, and dollar movies. When they're allowed to do so, kids can be very creative and can come up with long lists. They can also help create low-cost, healthy meal menus. Put all children in charge of at least one meal a week: let them decide what to cook, help do the shopping, and then cook (or help cook) the meal.

It all sounds easy, but life in the real world is often anything but. Jenny was a single mom who worked as a paralegal. Jenny had two children, aged eight and eleven; their father hadn't given her any child support in over six months, and the small salary she received each week didn't cover her bills. Feeling overwhelmed and afraid had become a way of life.

Jenny had gone to the district attorney about collecting her child support payments, but there were no guarantees of payment. Not knowing where else to turn, she let her boss know that she was very disappointed that she was not making enough money to pay her bills. She threatened to look for another job. Her boss (also a single parent) knew Jenny was receiving a fair salary for her skill level and was neither able nor willing to pay her more. Jenny's boss began to think about looking for a new paralegal.

Jenny's feelings of being overwhelmed and her ineffective way of expressing them almost cost her her job. Being unemployed would certainly have been more overwhelming than having a job that didn't quite pay the bills.

What were the options for Jenny? She could have looked for a higher-paying job; however, it was doubtful that her skills were good enough to merit a better salary. Or she could have taken a closer look at her situation to see if budgeting would help. As it happened, Jenny was spending a large portion of her income on clothes and a new car. She was an excellent example of someone caught in the trap of materialism. Jenny's expectations and her reality were far apart.

Financial worries often come from the belief—or the reality—that we don't have enough of what we need. This in turn creates a feeling of deprivation. Changing a feeling can be a difficult task, but recognizing an attitude is the first step to changing it. Feelings of scarcity often lead to self-pity and blaming, which usually hamper productivity.

Jenny was feeling deprived and afraid, and it was hindering her productivity at work and her ability to see solutions for her financial problems. Once she recognized her feelings, she was ready for the next step. She began by making a budget. She wrote down all her necessities: food, shelter, basic clothing, and transportation. Then she looked at her necessity budget and decided where that could be cut. She decided to find a housemate to help pay the rent. She and the kids started planning meals together and decided they could eat out only twice a month instead of twice a week. Jenny had purchased an "ego" car that was expensive to maintain. She sold that car and bought a used car—one that had a reputation for needing little maintenance.

Jenny also made a vow that she wouldn't use her charge cards any more. She made a plan to pay them off and to purchase things only if she had the cash to pay for them—and only after necessities were taken care of. An important part of Jenny's new direction was to focus on improving her skills as a paralegal. She started taking one class each semester at a community college. She wanted to make sure that when her boss could afford to pay more, she would be eligible for a raise.

Your Attitude Is the Key

Have you ever noticed those rare people who have very little, yet who live their lives with joy and gratitude? Then there are others who always want more, no matter how much they have. Happiness truly is based more on attitude than on circumstances. Develop an attitude of gratitude for what you have. Not only will you be happier, but you'll have a kind of positive energy that will help you create abundance in your life — and in the lives of those around you.

It's difficult to view hard times as opportunities and problems as challenges to be conquered, but remember that your children will be quick to follow your lead. If your attitude is one of deprivation and "Oh, poor me," your children will be likely to adopt this perspective. However, if you work at keeping a positive attitude and remaining open to learning beneficial skills, your children are likely to catch your spirit.

This does not mean you won't be tested. Your children (and you) will be bombarded by television commercials designed to brainwash you into materialism. Your children will be faced with the "name brand" mentality of their peers. You may want to have more discussions with them to help them learn to think for themselves instead of falling for the brainwashing attempts that surround them.

Learning to budget wisely and to handle the demands of a job will help you bring one of the biggest pressures of single parenthood under control. But what about parenting itself? Can we do an adequate job in one area of our lives without neglecting another?

Learning to Lean: Building a Support Network

Being a single parent often can seem like being the Lone Ranger, only without Tonto and Silver. There's so much to be done and so little help—or so it seems. Carla, a talented professional woman with a growing career, had been a single mom for most of her six-year-old daughter's life. Ashley was a wonderful child, bright, friendly, and busy, but sometimes she could be *such* a handful. So, when Carla walked into her friend Alice's kitchen one afternoon, the tears seemed to come out of nowhere.

"I love my daughter more than anyone in the world," Carla explained after she'd calmed down a bit, "but I hate parenting sometimes. It feels like a trap. I just don't know how to be a good parent and still have a life of my own."

"You sound pretty overwhelmed," Alice said gently. "What's going on?"

Carla sighed. "I feel like I don't have time for myself or for the things I need to do. I'm always having to pick Ashley up from school or take her somewhere. Getting child care is such a hassle, and then I worry that no one else will take care of my daughter the way I do, or that I should be spending more time with her. And the more frustrated I feel, the more controlling and impatient I get with Ashley. I feel like crawling into a closet —in fact, I guess that's what I do. I'm ashamed to talk about the way I feel. I want to be such a good parent, and so often I'm not."

Alice smiled at her friend. "You know," she said, "I bet you're not the only one who feels this way. I heard about a parenting class for single parents—maybe it's worth checking out."

Carla was skeptical, but she figured that anything was worth a try. And so, one evening, she found herself sitting in a room full of other single parents, who were saying many of the things she herself had said and thought and felt. "I'm *not* alone," she realized. "And maybe there are ways to work through everything I'm feeling."

Since it takes two to create a child, it seems to follow that parenting was meant to be a partnership. Sometimes when that partnership is no longer available, single parents feel they must be both mother and father to their children. So, in addition to the stresses of running a home, providing a living, and taking care of children, harried single parents find themselves trying to fill a double role: playing ball with a son, dolls with a daughter, cooking, sewing, coaching, helping with carpentry projects, being a pal and a parent and a teacher. If you can do all of those things without raising a sweat, congratulations. But is it really necessary?

An important part of dealing with the overwhelming pressures of being a single parent may be allowing your child's other parent, if he or she is available, to play his or her part in your child's life. While that may be an emotionally difficult thing to do (see Chapter 11), it may be the best thing for your child in the long run—and it may take some of the burden off you. Even if your child's other parent isn't in the picture, it's enough if you are simply yourself: one parent, doing the best job you can.

There are times when two heads are better than one, when you need a safety net to fall back on. And there are ways to go about building a support system for yourself.

Businessmen have long known the value of networking. Doctors frequently recommend a second opinion. And single parents have a special need for a network—people who can offer advice, help, skills, another perspective. It's a wonderful thing when you realize that you don't have to know everything—you only need to know who to ask. But how do you find out who to ask? How does a single parent go about building a support network?

1. Check your community for parenting classes. They are not only wonderful places to learn new skills, but

they're also places to meet other parents, some of whom may be in similar situations and who may have discovered solutions to your problems. Parenting classes also allow you to realize that you're not alone — and sometimes that can make all the difference.

2. Keep your eyes and ears open, and don't be afraid to ask for help. A neighbor may be glad to help out with batting practice; an older woman at church may be thrilled to teach your child to knit or sew. A co-worker with children of the same ages may be able to help with ideas, child care, or transportation. And friends may have expertise in areas you don't: home repair, gardening, sports. Ask and see what happens.

3. When possible, keep relationships with grandparents, aunts, uncles and other family members strong. Even if you're no longer related by marriage, family members can remain a wonderful source of advice and nurturing. And it helps children to heal when they know they still belong to their extended family. When it isn't possible to maintain existing family relationships, create a new "extended family" with friends and support groups.

4. Save time for friendships. Friends are not only wonderful listeners, but they can be sources of wisdom as well as great problem-solvers. Don't be afraid to talk about what you're experiencing and feeling with people who care.

5. Check in your local area for single-parent organizations, such as Parents Without Partners. If there are none, consider starting one yourself. Beginning a group only takes one other single parent who is willing to be open, and you may find your group growing by leaps and bounds as other single parents realize its value and the opportunities it creates. Your local family service agency may be able to give you referrals.

6. If you're divorced, don't write off your ex-spouse. Your relationship with your child's other parent can be complicated and emotional — but sometimes that parent will see an aspect of a situation that you've missed, or may know a more effective way of dealing with a problem than the ones you've tried. Learning to listen, and learning that you don't have to be right all the time, is occasionally humbling — but it's liberating too.

"Mom," seven-year-old Cody yelled as he burst through the door after a weekend with his dad. "Come out here — I've got a surprise for you!"

As she followed her excited son into the garage, Janet wondered what could have happened. She was flabbergasted when Cody climbed onto his bicycle, wobbled just a little, and rode proudly off down the street, flashing her a grin you could read by on a dark night.

The bicycle had become a difficult topic for Janet and Cody. All the other children in the neighborhood had been riding for months, but Cody couldn't seem to learn. Janet had tried everything she could think of to help, but a few bad falls had shaken Cody's confidence, and each time he realized he was on his own, the teetering began. Nothing worked — not practice sessions, not running alongside him, not encouragement, not ignoring the whole thing. The bicycle had become larger than life.

Now, after a weekend with his dad, Cody was cruising proudly around the neighborhood. And as Janet watched him, she began to wonder what had made the difference.

It turned out that Dad had bought him a bike to keep at Dad's house, and the miracle had occurred when they went to try it out. "What did Dad do that I didn't?" Janet asked her son.

Cody thought for a moment or two. "Well," he said, "he didn't tell me when he let go of me. And he taught me how to crash."

Janet was floored. She never would have thought of those things, but they had made all the difference in the world. Cody had possessed the skills he needed to ride a bike all along; what he'd lacked was confidence. Learning that he could survive his crashes had given him the courage to try again. Janet felt an odd mixture of joy for her son and disappointment that she hadn't been the one to help him, but as she watched him circling with his friends she decided to be grateful that Cody's dad had done what she could not.

Janet and Cody both learned a valuable lesson—learning to crash successfully is a pretty important part of life. Being a single parent can be frightening. We feel responsible for our children, for their well-being, for their happiness. We feel we should always know what to do—and so often we simply don't. One of the most important assets we can acquire is the courage to risk "crashing," to learn we can fail or lose our dreams and still survive. Sometimes we're even stronger for the experience.

It helps to know that our inadequacies and failures as parents need not be permanent. Parents can't be perfect, no matter how hard we try, but children don't need perfect parents. They only need parents who love and accept them, who are willing to learn and do the best they can.

Being a single parent can be overwhelming. It can also be an exciting opportunity to build special relationships with our children. Budgeting our time and money and learning to find help when we need it will make single parenting less stressful and more joyous with each passing day.

CHAPTER 5

Understanding Misbehavior

Adjusting to single parenthood can take time. But once you've dealt with the changes and organized your life as best you can, the basic issues of raising children—and dealing with their misbehavior—still remain. "I've worked through most of my feelings," you may be saying, "and my life seems to be running pretty smoothly most of the time. Now how do I handle these children? And what do I do when they misbehave?"

It's important to remember that any problems you may be having with your children are probably pretty normal. There are no perfect kids and no perfect parents, and it's unlikely that hassles occur just because you're a single parent. Many newly divorced parents believe every misbehavior is directly related to the divorce when that may not be the case at all. *All* parents struggle with their children from time to time, and *all* children misbehave. Learning to interpret children's feelings and behavior can be difficult for any parent, but there are clues in everything our children do (and in how we respond). Once you know how to read the clues, dealing with the behavior becomes much easier.

Sandy is a single parent who runs a day-care program in her home. She has two children of her own, four-year-old Kyle and six-year-old Joey. Sandy told her parenting group that she needed help. Near tears, she reported that Joey was driving her crazy while she tried to manage the day-care program. "He taunts the younger children, hits them, takes their toys, and uses nasty language. He fights with the older boys over the use of the equipment. Joey's not having this trouble at school or at his friends' homes. He only misbehaves with me. He's so bad that I want to stop having the children come right now and give him the attention he needs. I think the day-care is too hard for him to handle because I'm a single mom and he doesn't want to share me with so many other kids. He's constantly saying I'm unfair."

Sandy continued to share: She had told Joey she would stop running the day-care in June. She couldn't stop sooner because of her obligations to the families who counted on her, and because she needed the money to help support her family. She hadn't figured out how she would earn money when she gave up the day-care, but Joey was her primary concern.

The parenting group facilitator asked, "Do you want to give up your day-care business?"

Sandy answered, "No, I love it, but Joey is more important. I want peace and harmony between us and I worry about his self-esteem."

The facilitator smiled. "Would you be willing to look at some possibilities that could help you continue the day-care, create peace and harmony between you and Joey, and improve his self-esteem?"

Sandy didn't hesitate. "Of course I would!"

"Okay, then," said the facilitator. "Let's look at some basics first, then we'll work on some suggestions. Is it fair that you should have to stop your day-care because Joey can't handle it? Could you do this without some hidden resentment?"

Sandy thought a moment. "No, probably not. I just don't know what else to do."

"Who's in control if you do give up your day-care even though you don't want to?" the facilitator asked.

"Well, obviously Joey is." Sandy shrugged. "I know that isn't healthy, but I can't think what else to do. He obviously needs my attention."

The facilitator continued, "What message are you sending to Joey by allowing him to manipulate you with his emotions?"

Now Sandy smiled wearily. "That he can be a total tyrant — and that's what it feels like to me. I'm so confused. I love him and want to be a good mother, but I will feel resentful if I give in to him and give up a job I love and can do at home. Having a day-care program in my home seemed like the perfect way to earn money without having to leave my kids. But the dream has turned into a nightmare."

The facilitator turned to the group. "It's time for some brainstorming. Let's see how many ideas we can come up with that could help Sandy and Joey."

The group came up with a long list of ideas Sandy could try. She was invited to choose the one she would feel most comfortable with. Sandy heard so many good ideas, however, that she chose a combination of several of them:

1. Meet with Joey at a calm time and use the Four Steps for Winning Cooperation. (We'll explain these shortly.)

2. Let Joey have some things that he doesn't have to share with anyone.

3. Spend special time alone with Joey (and with Kyle).

4. Give Joey some jobs so he can feel he's making an important contribution and can also earn some extra money.

5. Get Joey involved in finding solutions to problems so he'll feel he belongs and is significant.

6. Reach out for support by talking to someone in a similar situation who can share his or her experience.

Sandy started with the last suggestion. She called Betty, from the day-care association, and shared her problem. Betty laughed and said, "Am I ever glad I'm over that one! I had the same problem when my kids were younger. I think it's very normal. It's hard for kids to share their moms, even when they aren't single moms. Two things helped me. I wouldn't play the 'no fair' game, so my kids didn't hook me with that one. But I did allow them to have toys that were their own and didn't have to be shared with anyone. The other thing was letting them know how much I enjoyed making a good living while still being with them. It helped them to see the benefits as well as the problems."

Sandy was encouraged—and relieved—to hear that her problem was normal and wasn't happening just because she was a single mom. All kids need attention, but Sandy was giving Joey attention in a way that invited unhealthy manipulation. She realized that she had fallen into the trap of trying to "make it up to her kids" because they didn't have a father. It was a relief to give up that belief and all the guilt that went with it.

After talking to Betty, Sandy felt validated for her desire to make a living in a way that included spending time with her kids. She felt encouraged in her belief that it was a worthwhile endeavor. Betty had made enough money to stay home with her children, and even enough to help put them through college. Betty said, "Of course there were some problems and some hassles, but what job *doesn't* include some problems? The benefits far outweighed them."

By reaching out for support, Sandy learned the importance of filling her own cup—getting strength and encouragment—before she could fill Joey's cup and resolve the problem. She was able to work with Joey on positive solutions because she was able to drop her misplaced guilt. Now that she was ready, Sandy decided to start with the Four Steps for Winning Cooperation.

The Four Steps for Winning Cooperation

1. Get into the child's world and make a guess about what he or she might be feeling. (If you're wrong, guess again.)

2. Show understanding. (Sometimes it helps to describe a time when you felt the same.)

3. Ask your child if he or she is willing to listen to your feelings. (Children listen better when they have agreed.)

4. Work on a solution together. (The first two steps create a feeling of closeness and trust so children will be more willing to listen and to work on solutions in a cooperative manner.)

Sandy was glad to see that Joey was still awake when she got home from her parenting class. Kyle had already fallen asleep. It was a perfect, calm time to try the Four Steps for Winning Cooperation. Sandy started by asking Joey, "Honey, could we have a special talk just between me and you while I'm tucking you into bed?"

"Yeah, okay," Joey replied.

Sandy continued, "I was wondering if you feel like you aren't important to me when I'm running the day-care."

Sandy had struck a nerve. Joey replied angrily, "It's not fair that I have to share all my stuff."

Now Sandy reflected and validated his feelings. She offered her understanding — and a story of her own. "I can see how you'd feel that way. I can remember when I was a little girl and my mom made me share all my clothes with my younger sister — even my favorites. I hated it. I can see now that by trying to be fair to all the other kids, I was very unfair to you. I made you share your dinnertime chair even when you tried to tell me you didn't think it was fair. I'm so sorry I didn't consider your feelings. I'll try to do better from now on."

Joey felt understood. He was touched by his mother's admission and apology, and he started to cry. "I'm sorry for being so bad." (Children often cry from relief when they feel understood. And when a parent takes responsibility for disrespectful behavior, it frees children to do the same.)

Sandy reassured Joey. "Honey, you aren't bad. We both made some mistakes. I'll bet we can work on some solutions together. First, would you be willing to hear some of my feelings?"

Joey sniffled. "Okay," he said.

Sandy drew Joey close to her. "You're more important to me than any job. And I'd really like to keep the day care so I don't have to go to work outside our home. I like being able to work and be with you at the same time. Would you be willing to help find some ways that we can do this? I know you have some great ideas that I haven't listened to before. I'd really like to hear them now."

Joey grinned. "Okay!"

Together, Sandy and Joey came up with the following plans: Joey and Sandy would spend 15 minutes of special time together every day with no phones, no little brother, and no other children. Joey agreed that Kyle should have the same amount of time and that they could all work together to agree on the times that would be convenient. During a family meeting they would brainstorm suggestions for what each could do while the other was spending special time with Mom. Joey was enthusiastic about the possibility of helping out and earning some extra money. They agreed that he would earn $1.00 every day by making all the lunches for the day-care children. He volunteered to take on other jobs, like picking up toys. They also decided that no one else could sit in his dinner chair unless he gave permission. They ended their talk by agreeing that in the future, if something was bothering them, they would talk about it and work together on solutions that felt respectful to all concerned.

Sandy was ecstatic at her next parenting group. "I can't believe how well this stuff works! Joey is now helping and seems to feel great about himself instead of misbehaving. At our family meeting he told Kyle how lucky they are to have a mom who can work at home. When I got Joey involved in problem solving, he had so many good ideas. I'm so glad that I got to tell him how much I love him, and that he could really hear me. Thank you all so much!"

Sandy found a way to get out of the win/lose struggle. It wouldn't have been healthy for Joey to "win" at Sandy's expense, nor for Sandy to "win" at Joey's expense. Control is not an issue when we learn to "win" cooperation *with* our children.

Both Sandy and Joey had an underlying belief that he was being "bad." Children are never bad—but they're often discouraged. And when they're discouraged, they misbehave.

Understanding the Code

Misbehaving children are using a code to tell us what they're feeling and experiencing. Misbehavior is a coded message that says, "I'm discouraged because I don't believe that I'm important or that I'm loved unconditionally."

Children are not consciously aware of these beliefs, nor do they know that their misbehavior is a way of telling us they're discouraged. It's not important that they know. It *is* important that parents realize there *is* a belief behind every behavior.

Beliefs Behind Behavior

Dealing with the belief behind the behavior does not mean you don't deal with the behavior, but you will be most successful when you are aware of both factors.

What happens to us is never as important as the decisions and beliefs we create *about* what happens to us. Our behavior is then based on those decisions and beliefs. The decisions and beliefs we form are directly related to the primary goal of all people: our need to find belonging and significance.

The Primary Goal of All People

We all want to belong somewhere, to someone, and to feel significant, worthwhile and loved. From the moment they first become aware of their surroundings, children are making decisions about whether they belong, whether they're loved, whether they're accepted. Sometimes children decide they don't belong (which might surprise their parents), and then they make unconscious decisions about what they need to do about it. Sometimes those decisions involve misbehavior; sometimes they result in an unwillingness to try at all.

Kevin was a sadly neglected little boy — so neglected, in fact, that when his mother's house in a rural town caught fire, his older brother was carried to safety but he was left in his bed to be rescued at the last minute by a diligent fireman. His unmarried mother was pregnant and didn't want him; his grandmother took his older brother, but she didn't want Kevin. When he arrived at Paula's home as a foster child, he could barely walk, although he was almost two, and he couldn't talk, except to say "bite-bite" when he was hungry.

A brief four months later, Kevin was walking and running, delighting in giving and getting hugs, and chattering constantly. "He called me Mama a week after he arrived," Paula said. What had made the difference? "We just told him over and over that he was special to us and that we loved him."

Is it really that simple? Our children, like all humans, need some very basic things from their parents (besides food, shelter, and clothing). They need to feel accepted, to know they belong, and to be sure that they're special and worthy of love just as they are.

"Well, of course I love my kids," we say, feeling faintly offended that anyone would question that. Yet too often we fail to communicate that love to our children in a way that is meaningful. We fail to separate the child from his behavior, letting him believe that when he messes up, we don't love him as much. "Bad boy!" we may say. "You'll never amount to anything." Or we reserve our love and encouragement for the times when our child achieves something, letting her believe that love and acceptance must be earned. And setting children up to need approval and acceptance from others is just asking for trouble later down the road.

We must learn, hard as it seems at times, to accept our children just as they are, not only as we wish they would be. We can let them know that while there may be room for improvement in certain areas, they don't have to become someone else for us to love them, that our love has no strings and no conditions. We can give them the security of knowing that no matter how rough a situation seems, Mom and Dad care and will be there. We can let them know that we love them, no matter what.

What Happens When We Don't Feel the Love and Belonging?

All of us, parents and children alike, are active participants (not victims) in the process of deciding things about ourselves, about others, and about life, and our behavior is based on these decisions. Understanding this process— how your children create their beliefs about life and how they fit into their family— is the first step to understanding their behavior. With this understanding, you can encourage your kids— and provide opportunities for them to change their unhealthy beliefs and behaviors.

All of us seek ways to belong and be important. Sometimes they work and sometimes they don't. If we think we aren't loved or don't belong, we usually try to do something to get the love back. Or we hurt others to get revenge when we think they don't love us. Sometimes we even feel like giving up; it seems impossible to do things right, to belong, to be loved and accepted. The things we do when we believe we don't belong and aren't important are often mistaken ways of seeking the acceptance we need. That is why they are called the Four Mistaken Goals of Misbehavior.

The Four Mistaken Goals of Misbehavior[1]

There are four different reasons—four goals—children can have for misbehaving. They are:

1. Undue Attention: "I belong only when you pay constant attention to me."

2. Power: "I belong only if I'm the boss, or, at least, if I don't let you boss me."

3. Revenge: "I feel hurt and can find belonging only if I hurt back."

4. Assumed Disability: "I don't believe I can belong, and I just want to give up."

Children are not aware of these hidden beliefs. They don't sit down and plan a power struggle. But once *we* understand their reasons for behaving as they do, we can think of ways to encourage them when they're feeling discouraged—and to change their behavior in the process.

The Mistaken Goal Chart (at the end of this chapter) helps you identify the mistaken goal of your misbehaving child and offers some suggestions for encouraging him or her.

---

1. Mistaken Goal charts and more information on the "Four Mistaken Goals of Misbehavior" can be found in *Positive Discipline* (Ballantine, 1981) by Jane Nelsen and *I'm On Your Side: Resolving Conflict with Your Teenage Son or Daughter* (Prima, 1991) by Jane Nelsen and Lynn Lott, to be revised and re-released as *Positive Discipline for Teenagers* (Prima, 1994).

The first step is to identify the way the misbehavior makes *you* feel. For example, if you're feeling irritated, that's a clue that your child's goal is attention. The second clue comes from noticing your child's response to your usual ways of dealing with his misbehavior. If your child's mistaken goal is power, for example, and you use power to respond, the misbehavior will escalate. The rest of the chart describes the belief behind each mistaken goal and some empowering ways to respond.

When we understand our children's thinking, their beliefs about themselves, about others, and about life, we're in a better position to influence them in positive ways. We're much more effective when we deal with the belief behind the behavior instead of the behavior alone.

Remember Joey and Sandy? Joey felt unimportant and insignificant until Sandy used the Four Steps for Winning Cooperation, which helped Joey come to some new conclusions. As soon as he believed he belonged and was significant, he was open to the encouragement his mom offered by hearing his feelings, sharing hers, and working with him on solutions. Learning to understand the hidden code in Joey's misbehavior gave Sandy the information she needed to help him form different beliefs, give up his misbehavior, and become part of a cooperative team.

Our children's behavior — good, bad, and indifferent — doesn't happen in a vacuum. It's a result of the way they're feeling about themselves, about us, and about their place in life. Misbehavior can be annoying and irritating, but understanding these feelings — and the code your children use to communicate them to you — may be all you need to solve the problem. Children who feel encouraged, loved, and worthwhile have less need to misbehave. And isn't that what we're really after?

MISTAKEN GOAL CHART

If the **Parent/Teacher** feels:	And tends to **React** by:	And if the **Child's Response** is:	The **Child's Goal** is:
Annoyed Irritated Worried Guilty	Reminding Coaxing Doing things for the child he/she could do for him/herself	Stops temporarily, but later resumes same or another disturbing behavior	Undue attention (to keep others busy or to get special service)
Angry Provoked Challenged Threatened Defeated	Fighting Giving in Thinking: "You can't get away with it." "I'll make you." Wanting to be right	Intensifies behavior Defiant compliance Feels he/she has won when parents/teachers are upset Passive power	Power (to be boss)
Hurt Disappointed Disbelieving Disgusted	Retaliating Getting even Thinking: "How could you do this to me?"	Retaliates Intensifies Escalates the same behavior or chooses another weapon	Revenge (to get even)
Despair Hopeless Helpless	Giving up Doing for Overhelping	Retreats further Passive No improvement No response	Assumed disability (to give up and be left alone)

The BELIEF behind the CHILD'S BEHAVIOR is:	PARENT/TEACHER ALTERNATIVES include:
I count (belong) only when I'm being noticed or getting special service. I'm only important when I'm keeping you busy with me.	"I love you and ____." (Example: I care about you and will spend time with you later.) Give positive attention at other times. Avoid special service. Say it only once, then act. Plan special time. Set up routines. Take time for training. Use natural and logical consequences. Encourage. Redirect. Use family/class meetings. Touch without words. Ignore. Set up nonverbal signals.
I belong only when I'm boss or in control, or proving no one can boss me. "You can't make me."	Ask for help. Don't fight and don't give in. Withdraw from conflict. Do the unexpected. Be firm and kind. Act, don't talk. Decide what you will do. Let routines be the boss. Leave and calm down. Develop mutual respect. Give limited choices. Set reasonable and few limits. Practice follow through. Encourage. Redirect to positive power. Use family/class meetings.
I don't think I belong so I'll hurt others as I feel hurt. I can't be liked or loved.	Deal with the hurt feelings. Avoid feeling hurt. Avoid punishment and retaliation. Build trust. Use reflective listening. Share your feelings. Make amends. Show you care. Act, don't talk. Encouragement of strengths. Put kids in same boat. Use family/class meetings.
I can't belong because I'm not perfect, so I'll convince others not to expect anything of me. I am helpless and unable; it's no use trying because I won't do it right.	Show faith. Take small steps. Stop all criticism. Encourage any positive attempt, no matter how small. Focus on assets. Don't pity. Don't give up. Set up opportunities for success. Teach skills/show how. Step back. Enjoy the child. Build on their interests. Encourage, encourage, encourage. Use family/class meetings.

CHAPTER 6

Get into Your Child's World

As parents we have *such* good intentions. We want our children to be well-behaved "for their own good." Their ultimate happiness is our main concern, and we know they won't be happy if they don't adopt our wonderful values and do what is right. We really believe that our lectures, punishments, and shaming will help them behave better and adopt our values — the correct ones. We know what we want to teach our children. The trouble is that we seldom take the time to check out what they're learning. We don't ask them what they're feeling, what they're thinking, and what they're deciding.

Beware of What Works

We may be fooled into thinking our methods are working when we punish a child for a certain behavior and the behavior stops. Sometimes, though, we need to *beware of what works*. Suppose you've punished a child for "talking back" and she stops talking back. It may appear that the punishment has worked. What you may not know is that she's feeling hurt and confused; she's thinking you're unfair and don't really care about her; and she's deciding that you can make her stop talking back, but you can't make her do well in school. The long-range effect of "what worked" is revenge. You've just won one battle—and changed the direction of the entire war.

And war it is. Lectures, punishments, and shaming are just a few of the weapons parents use against their children for the "good cause" of helping them behave well and adopt good values. The casualties of this war are discouraged children with low self-esteem—children who haven't been listened to and taken seriously, and who haven't learned to develop their own wisdom and problem-solving skills. These children don't have a sense of belonging and significance. Some of them act out and rebel. Others become "pleasers," finding friends and spouses who will continue to tell them what to do.

Sheila is a single parent who wanted to end the war with her three children. She decided to get some help by attending a parenting class, where she learned about the importance of getting into the child's world. She had an opportunity to practice some of the skills she'd learned when she discovered that her son Casey, an eighth-grader, had been suspended from school for calling the teacher names.

When Sheila walked into the den, she found Casey sitting in front of the television set with a belligerent look on his face. Sheila took a deep breath and asked, "Casey, could we talk about the problem you're having at school?"

Casey looked up from his program and reluctantly said, "Yeah, I guess."

Sheila fought back the urge to dive right into the problem. She smiled. "I can tell you're not real excited to talk to me about this. I'll bet it's because you're used to hearing lectures from me instead of having us really talk and listen to each other."

Now Sheila had her son's attention. He was obviously surprised to hear his mother admit she lectured. She noticed his interest and continued with a laugh, "I confess. I'm guilty of lecturing and not listening. I really don't want to do that anymore. I'll bet you feel like I don't really care about you when I lecture and scold. The truth is that I care very much. Would you give me another chance so I can show you that talking with each other doesn't always have to include lectures or judgments from me?"

Casey didn't know what to think now. This was new territory. It felt nice to have his mom be so understanding, but he wasn't sure he could trust this new approach. He answered again, hesitantly, "Yeah, I guess."

Sheila relaxed a bit. She said gently, "Tell me what's going on from your point of view. I really want to hear your side of the story."

Casey was still uncertain. He decided to take refuge in his television program. "It's okay, Mom," he said, turning his gaze back to the TV. "I can handle it."

Sheila felt a surge of compassion for her son. Her love for him began giving her clues on how to proceed. She put all of her love for Casey into her voice and said calmly, "I'm sure you can, one way or another. But I'd still like to hear your side of what happened."

Casey looked up and met his mother's eyes. There was a pause, and then he blurted out, "Those teachers are jerks. They don't like me." Now there was anger in his voice.

"Could you give me an example of what you mean?" his mother replied. "What do they do to act like jerks and give you the impression that they don't like you?"

This was getting a bit uncomfortable for Casey, and he retreated again. "Don't worry about it. I can handle it." After a moment, he added in a quiet voice, "I've already decided I don't want to get kicked out of school."

Sheila tried not to let her relief show too much. "Frankly, I'm glad that's important to you. *You're* important to me, and I'd still like to know what's really going on from your point of view. I have some hunches. I don't know if they're right, but would it be okay with you if I make some guesses? I have more than one guess. You can let me know if I'm off base. Okay?"

Goal Disclosure

Sheila had begun a process developed by Rudolf Dreikurs[1] called "goal disclosure." During this process an adult makes guesses to discover the child's mistaken goal. When done in a friendly manner goal disclosure can help a child feel understood. Children are not conciously aware of their mistaken goal, and awareness can be the beginning of change. The four steps of goal disclosure are:

1. Ask the child "why" he or she is doing a specific behavior. Be ready for the usual answer: "I don't know."

2. Ask permission to guess why. Most children will give permission if you have demonstrated friendliness and genuine caring.

3. Ask, "Could it be _____?" regarding each mistaken goal until you get a "yes" or a recognition reflex. This occurs when a child says "no" but can't suppress a smile or some other involuntery reaction. (The smile is saying "yes" while the voice says "no.") When you get a recognition reflex, respond by saying, "You say 'no,' but your smile tells me that could be the reason. Would you be willing to work with me on some solutions?"

4. Refer to the last column of the Mistaken Goal chart for some possible solutions and work together on other possibilities.

As we finish the story of Sheila and Casey you will see how Sheila continues to use the process of goal disclosure. Casey felt encouraged by Sheila's friendly manner. This allowed him to let down his defenses and become curious about her guesses.

---

1. Rudolf Dreikurs, *Children: The Challenge*, New York: E. P. Dutton, 1987.

However, his vocabulary hadn't improved. He said, "Yeah, I guess."

Sheila made her first attempt to discover what his mistaken goal might be. "Could it be that getting in trouble with the teachers is a good way to get my attention and make me spend some time with you?"

Casey's answer was prompt: "No way." (This eliminated the mistaken goal of attention.)

Sheila said, "Well, let me try another guess. Could it be that you're showing me that no one can boss you around or make you do anything you don't want to do?"

This guess got Sheila an exasperated sigh. "That would be a dumb reason for getting into trouble." (This eliminated the mistaken goal of power.)

Sheila paused for a moment. This was the hard one. "Could it be that you feel hurt and angry at me for divorcing your dad, and getting into trouble is a good way to hurt me back?"

Casey caught his breath. For a brief moment he looked as if he'd just been caught with his hand in the cookie jar. Then he asked defiantly, "Are you and Dad ever going to get back together?" (Casey's expression and his reply showed Sheila that she'd discovered the mistaken goal: revenge.)

Sheila sighed, and sat down next to her son. "Honey, I can see how much this has hurt you, and I'm so sorry. Your dad and I are not going to get back together. I wish it didn't have to hurt you so much, but I know it does. You don't have to keep it to yourself. You can tell me how angry you are. I promise to listen."

His mother's understanding had broken down Casey's inhibitions, and now he finally expressed what he felt. "If you hadn't been such a bitch to Dad, you could still be married."

Sheila felt stung, and tears came to her eyes. But she realized that to respond by defending herself or by striking back would close the door she and her son had just so painstakingly opened. "Ouch," she said quietly. "That one really hurt. You must really hate me sometimes."

Casey found tears in his own eyes as he struggled with the strong, complex emotions in his heart. He did hate his mom sometimes, but he also loved her a lot. Sheila guessed what he was feeling. She put her arms around him and said, "It's okay, honey. I know you love me too. It can be a real bind when you both hate and love someone." She laughed. "Sometimes I feel that way about you, too."

Casey seemed relieved. He didn't realize it, but he'd been feeling guilty and confused about his feelings. He hadn't known what to do with all his hurt and anger, but somehow his feelings didn't seem so bad when they were out in the open and he knew his mom sometimes felt the same way.

Sheila continued, "I can't change your feelings, and I don't want to. Everyone has a right to their feelings. I'd like to talk with you later about some things we could do to solve some of the problems that come up. Would you be willing to do that with me?"

Casey grinned. "Yeah, I guess," he said.

During this situation Sheila had used several principles she had learned in her Positive Discipline parenting class:

1. **Create a Foundation of Love and Closeness.** Sheila understood the importance of creating a foundation of love and closeness before she could have a positive influence on Casey. Lectures and punishment create distance and hostility, and the result is a negative influence. Most positive parenting tools are effective only after a foundation of love and closeness has been created.

   When we use a discipline method that doesn't produce positive results, the first question to ask is, "Are we engaged in a power struggle or a revenge cycle?" Sheila had asked herself this question and had thought she was in a power struggle with Casey. By taking the time to get into Casey's world, she found out that his goal was not power but revenge because of his hurt feelings about the divorce.

2. **Take Responsibility for Your Part in Creating the Problem.** Sheila took responsibility for her part in creating the problem (lecturing and not listening). Taking responsibility is not the same as accepting blame and guilt. Taking responsibility means gaining insight and awareness of what we create. When we become aware of what we're doing to create a situation, we'll also be aware that we can change it by doing something else. This is extremely empowering. When we take responsibility for our part, children will often follow our lead and become willing to take responsibility for their part. They, too, feel empowered.

3. **Ask for a Chance to Try Again.** By asking Casey if he would give her another chance to talk *with* him without lectures, Sheila was admitting that she had made a mistake and wanted to try again. What a beautiful model for children! They need to find out that mistakes are nothing more than opportunities to learn. They need to know that they can keep learning and keep trying, instead of thinking that mistakes mean failure so they might as well give up.

4. **Ask "What" and "How" Questions, and Ask for Examples to Facilitate Deeper Listening.** Sheila used effective listening skills to get to deeper levels by asking "what" questions and asking for examples. She avoided the temptation to lecture or moralize. Too often parents *tell* kids what happened, what caused it to happen, how they should feel about it, and what they should do about it. Kids feel belonging and significance when we *ask*, "What happened? What do you think caused that to happen? How do you feel about it? How would you like things to be? What could you do to make that happen?"

5. **Understand the Belief Behind the Behavior.** Sheila used *goal disclosure* (by making guesses to reveal the mistaken goal) to help both herself and Casey understand the *hidden* belief behind his behavior. Casey felt hurt and wanted to hurt back, even though he wasn't aware of it. All too often, parents deal with their children's symptoms (their problems and misbehavior) without understanding the causes (their beliefs and feelings). Taking time to understand a child's feelings may make a tremendous difference in your approach to a problem — and in your ability to find a solution.

6. **Validate Feelings.** Sheila validated Casey's feelings even when he said hurtful things to her. She understood the difference between feelings and actions, and asked Casey to work with her later on possible actions. Too often we forget that there's a difference between feelings and actions. We try to talk kids out of their feelings, or just plain tell them, "You shouldn't feel that way." Sometimes we try to rescue them, or to fix things, so they won't have to experience their feelings.

7. **Allow for a Cooling-Off Period Before Working on Solutions.** Some people may ask, "But what about the problem of Casey's suspension and his talking back to teachers?" Sheila was wise enough to know that simply disclosing the belief behind the behavior in a friendly, accepting manner is often enough to eliminate the misbehavior. When Casey feels better about himself and his mother (a process that this conversation helped to begin), he'll feel less need to get revenge. If the problem occurs again, Sheila has laid a foundation for problem solving that focuses on solutions instead of punishment.

8. **Discussion May Be Enough.** Too often we focus on consequences or solutions and underestimate the power of a friendly discussion that leads to

understanding. When children feel listened to, taken seriously, and loved, they may change the beliefs that motivated the misbehavior. For this reason, we end where we began: *Create a foundation of love and closeness.* It's the most important thing we can do to accomplish all our good intentions.

Mary had raised six children and had enjoyed being a parent. She had good relationships with all her grown children and looked forward to being a grandmother. She had fantasies that being a grandmother would be even more fun than being a parent because she could enjoy her grandchildren without all the day-to-day hassles. Then her daughter Lori got a divorce and, with her two boys, Cliff, 10, and Jake, 6, moved in with Mary.

So much for fantasies. Cliff was a defiant child who became sassy with his grandmother. When Mary asked him to do things around the house, he'd say, "This isn't my house. Clean it yourself." Mary got phone calls from teachers about his misbehavior at school. When she tried to talk to Cliff about it, he'd say, "That's none of your business."

Mary felt deeply hurt. She was trying to do so much for her grandchildren—giving them a home, caring about them and their behavior, trying to teach them responsibility as she'd taught her own children. Mary was a positive, loving person. She couldn't understand why Cliff would be so negative and hurtful to her.

Mary heard about a single parenting class and asked Lori if she would attend with her. Lori was also feeling discouraged about Cliff's behavior. They were both afraid Cliff would become a juvenile delinquent if they didn't get help.

At the first meeting Mary shared about how much children and parenting had changed. None of the six children she'd raised had ever hurt her so much. Of course she'd never had to deal with what she called the three Ds: Divorce, Defiance, and Drugs. (Mary was afraid drugs would be the next step for Cliff.)

The class leader agreed that times had changed, but pointed out that some things remain constant. One constant is that children still need to feel belonging and significance. They also want to be treated with dignity and respect, which may be a new concept for members of an older generation.

One theme of the class was *getting into the child's world* and dealing with the belief behind the behavior. A class member reminded Mary that we usually lash out at the ones we love. It might not have looked like love, but Cliff must have felt safe around her to strike out at her the way she described. Mary was excited and felt encouraged to try out her new insights and information.

At the next class she shared a wonderful story. During the week, Mary had focused on understanding Cliff's world. When she picked him up after school, she asked him some "what" and "how" questions in a spirit of honest inquiry instead of inquisition. "How are you feeling about school?" she began. After giving Cliff time to think and respond, she continued with sensitivity, "I'll bet it was hard for you to leave your friends and your home and move in with me."

Cliff could feel the energy of her honest caring. He opened up and shared with her his anger about what was happening to his life. He didn't like being a child of divorce. He didn't like it that his mother seemed to ignore him while she dealt with her own life. He felt he had no control. After expressing these feelings, he apologized for taking them out on Mary. "I know it isn't your fault," he said softly.

Mary responded, "I can only imagine how upsetting this must be for you. I don't know how I would deal with so much chaos in my life. It must really be tough."

Suddenly Cliff felt understood, and this gave him room to move in a different direction. He said, "I'll be okay. I can handle it."

Mary said, "I'll bet you can. I'd like to help in any way I can. I'm reading a book about family meetings where family members work together on solutions to problems, share feelings, and plan fun things to do together.[2] Your old family has changed, and now we have a different family. This family doesn't match our society's picture of the ideal family: a mom, a dad, and happy, obedient children. I hope you got that part about obedient children!" she joked. "But I'll bet we can do great things with the family we've got. What do you think?"

Cliff looked hopeful. "Yeah. Maybe."

As the parenting class progressed, Mary was able to tell the group, "I now have some tools to work with. They've helped me stop overreacting, get centered, and act more appropriately. My relationship with Cliff has really improved. He doesn't even try to hurt my feelings anymore because I don't bite the bait. I just focus on how hurt he must be feeling to act that way. He feels understood, and he changes his behavior. He helps around the house because he helped plan a chore schedule at the family meeting. We also focus on ways to make our family better. This doesn't mean things are perfect, but they're sure better than they were!"

"My relationship with my daughter Lori has also improved," Mary continued. "The funny thing was that as Cliff started getting better, Jake started misbehaving for a while. I was glad I'd been warned about this and knew that he might start misbehaving when he couldn't find belonging and significance by being the 'good' child. As we continued using family meetings and the other parenting tools we learned in the class, we all found belonging and significance through cooperation instead of competition."

Does getting into the child's world solve every problem? Of course not. But it gives parents valuable clues that help them understand why a behavior is occurring in the first place. And sometimes that can save a lot of energy—and a lot of anger and hurt feelings—down the road.

---

2. *Positive Discipline*, Jane Nelsen, Ballantine, 1981.

Getting into your child's world is about building a relationship of understanding, love, and trust. And that will do you and your children nothing but good on your journey as a family.

CHAPTER 7

Nonpunitive Discipline

Nonpunitive discipline: parents sometimes wonder if such a thing is possible, or even wise. Most of us have absorbed our ideas about discipline from our parents and from our society. And most of us have approached discipline with one subtle, basic belief: children have to suffer or they won't learn anything.

"I have to give my kids a swat once in a while to let them know I mean business," a parent might say. Or, "My children lose all their privileges when they mess up. That's what teaches them not to disobey me." Or, "Punishing my kids teaches them to respect me." The Bible says, "Spare the rod and spoil the child." Many people interpret this to mean spanking is mandated by God. (Biblical scholars tell us the rod was used to "guide" sheep, not to hit them.) Single parents in particular can find discipline a challenge. "Now that I'm alone," they say, "I have to keep a firmer grip on these kids or they'll run wild. You know what they say about kids from broken homes."

Parents often believe in the necessity of controlling their children, failing to realize that total control is not only unwise, it's rarely even possible — especially when children have grown too large to be physically moved and confined. Relying on control and the power of punishment turns parents into policemen, full-time enforcers who set the rules and then watch constantly for violations. But what happens when the policeman isn't around? What happens when teenagers go off with their friends? And what happens when family life seems to turn into a constantly escalating power struggle?

True discipline is not about punishment or control. The word itself comes from the Latin word *disciplina*, which means "teaching" or "learning." And at its best, discipline is about teaching and guiding, helping young people to make wise decisions about their behavior and to accept responsibility for their choices and actions — to choose (or not choose) a certain behavior because they understand its consequences, not because a policeman is lurking around the corner.

All parents must eventually ask themselves what they believe about discipline. If we believe that *we* are responsible for our children's behavior, that misbehavior deserves to be punished, and that children must suffer in order to learn, we'll find ourselves relying on spanking, grounding, and, all too often, a lot of anger. If, however, we believe that the purpose of discipline is to teach children responsibility for their *own* actions, to find a solution to a problem, and to keep that problem from happening in the future, we will approach discipline — and our children — much differently. But how?

The Perils of Punitive Discipline

The question of how we choose to discipline our children cuts to the heart of what we believe about parenting. Most of us grew up accepting that spanking and punishment were normal, even necessary, parts of raising children. And, at least in the short term, punishment seems to work well enough. But sometimes we need to beware of what seems to work for the moment, and consider the long-term effects of punitive discipline.

A recent segment of the ABC television news show "20/20" took a close look at spanking. Four families in which children are regularly spanked allowed the television cameras to follow them around and to record the parents' encounters with their misbehaving children. Most parents who viewed that show, including parents who had spanked their own children, found it painful to watch. Many agreed that the purpose of the spankings was almost always simply to punish a child for a wrong choice or to vent parental anger and frustration — there was no emphasis on problem solving or on changing future behavior. The spankings alone were supposed to take care of that.

Yet these parents kept having to spank their children regularly. There appeared to be no lasting changes in the undesirable behaviors. Perhaps more important, the show found that spanking and similar punishments produce children who have lower self-esteem, who may seek out abusive relationships, and who consider violence an acceptable way to solve problems — results that these parents, who certainly loved their children, obviously didn't intend.

Children who live with punitive forms of discipline frequently learn unintended lessons: to misbehave whenever the enforcer isn't around, to get even whenever possible, or to focus on the "mean old parent" rather than on the behavior that got them into trouble. Spanking, in particular, presents several hidden problems. It becomes less and less effective over time, and it eventually becomes physically impossible. Is it possible to do things another way?

Preventing the Problems

If discipline truly is about teaching and training rather than just punishment, a large part of effective discipline will be focused on creating an atmosphere of cooperation, taking into account children's abilities and limitations, and working together to prevent problems before they happen. For instance, if waiting quietly in a doctor's office or a restaurant is a problem for your child, be sure to talk *before you go* about acceptable behavior — and take along a bag filled with small toys or books, or invent a game to play. A little planning on a parent's part can make even the longest car trip bearable for everyone: a personal tape player and some story tapes, coloring books and crayons, or a few small, inexpensive new toys can save the day. If the child still misbehaves in a restaurant, quietly take her by the hand, and kindly and firmly take her to the car to wait while the others in your group finish their meal. Come prepared with a good book to read while you wait. This discipline teaches the child an immediate result of misbehavior—losing the privilege of eating in a restaurant. When children misbehave in a car, pull over to the side of the road and read some more of your good book until they let you know they're ready to stop misbehaving.

Some parents object that *they* are being punished if they have to leave their unfinished meal and sit in the car with a child who may still be throwing a temper tantrum, or sit by the side of the road reading a book when they have so many other "important" things to do. Another way to look at this is that it may take a little time and a few sacrifices to effectively teach children. Parents who have been willing to make this small sacrifice once or twice have found that they were able to spend many happy hours in restaurants and cars with children who could count on their parents to follow through with kind and firm action.

To make sure children understand the difference between appropriate and inappropriate restaurant behavior, it can be fun to role-play—in other words, to play "let's pretend"—with children three years old and older. Let them take turns playing a misbehaving child in a restaurant—they know how to do that! Then let them role play appropriate restaurant behavior. Be sure to let them know by your encouragement that the appropriate behavior is what you're looking for; make it more fun to behave well than to misbehave!

Sometimes "misbehavior" is exacerbated by expecting from children what they cannot give. Even the sweetest-natured toddler will become cranky after a full afternoon of errands, especially if nap-time has been disrupted, and expecting a young child to refrain from touching the pretty things in a gift shop, for example, is unrealistic. Getting down on a child's level, making eye contact, and explaining why we don't touch (or quietly, kindly, and firmly removing the child) is far more effective than allowing an accident to happen — and trying to cope with it afterwards.

It's always helpful to understand a child's (or a teenager's) development, and to know what they are and are not capable of at each age. It helps simply to know your own child. Some children enjoy airplane trips and need little preparation or planning, while others are afraid or overly energetic and need much more help finding acceptable ways to stay busy.

And remember: pick your battles carefully. Decide which issues are non-negotiable, and which you can compromise on. Every family will be different. Some parents value church attendance, while it's not important to others. Messy rooms push some parents' buttons while others couldn't care less. *Everything* can become a battle if we let it. Be sure you save your energy for the things that really matter.

Take Time to Teach

It's almost always better to prevent a problem than to have to react to one. Often problems can be averted by sitting down to talk, to explain, to check your child's understanding, and most important, to teach. Teaching your child just *how* you want the dishes washed (working alongside him is a good way) can avert later arguments about dishwashing; being sure your child knows *how* to operate the lawnmower safely will eliminate some of the reasons for not mowing the lawn.

It's important to teach problem-solving skills, too; children aren't born knowing how to resolve an argument. While ignoring sibling rivalry may work if the arguing is intended to get your attention (remember the mistaken goals?), an argument between children may continue indefinitely if children haven't been taught how to solve a problem or how to reach a compromise. And discussing rules in advance isn't nagging if it's done in a positive, respectful way—it's teaching and reinforcing, and it may just short-circuit a problem before it occurs. In the next chapter we'll discuss the importance of getting children involved in finding solutions through family meetings and brainstorming. This is one of the best ways to teach not only appropriate behavior, but critical life skills that will last a lifetime.

A Word to Noncustodial Parents

"But I hardly ever see my kids," you may be saying. "Their other parent is responsible for discipline most of the time. Does it really matter what I do? How much can I affect my kids when I only see them on weekends?"

Whether you're the custodial parent or not, the way you approach discipline with your children is important. You have the opportunity to create an environment in your own home that nurtures reponsibility in your children, regardless of how often you see them. Even one weekend a month in an atmosphere that is positive, encouraging, and respectful can have an influence, and it's important that all the time you spend with your children, whether it's a little or a lot, be the best you can make it. Giving some careful thought to the way you approach discipline may mean you have to spend less time actually *doing* it—and that leaves more time for fun!

Using Natural and Logical Consequences

Effective discipline structures a child's environment in such a way that he or she understands—in advance—the *consequences* of behavior. This will encourage children to use that knowledge in choosing what they'll do next time. For example, a natural consequence of failing to get enough sleep is feeling tired the next day. A child who has experienced being tired may be more willing to go to bed when asked—unless, of course, you turn the discussion into a power struggle by lecturing and scolding. A natural consequence of losing a toy is not to have the toy—and that painful lesson may be the best way to teach a child to be careful with possessions, especially if you show empathy for the child's feelings of disappointment instead of giving an "I told you so" lecture. Children can learn personal accountability from natural consequences only if parents avoid four traps:

Traps That Defeat Positive Effects of Natural Consequences

1. Blaming and shaming.

2. Adding punishment.

3. Fixing or rescuing.

4. Not showing empathy.

Parents can show empathy without falling into any of the first three traps by saying, "I can only imagine how bad you must feel." Period!

Adult interference (except the expression of empathy) is not necessary to allow children to learn from natural consequences. In fact, most adult interference is counterproductive. Sometimes a behavior has no natural consequence, however, or the natural consequence is unacceptable (the natural consequence of playing in the street, for instance). In that case, a parent can substitute a *logical* consequence. A logical consequence of failing to pick up toys could be losing the privilege of using those toys for a few days. Using natural and logical consequences is a wonderful way for parents to involve children in the process of discipline by focusing on future behavior, by talking with children about the results—good and bad—of the choices they make, and by setting up, ahead of time, the consequences that are reasonable, respectful, and related to the behavior.

For instance, when a child is constantly late for dinner, a parent can tell that child respectfully and kindly that dinner will be served at 6:00; if she chooses not to be home and ready to eat, the next meal served will be breakfast. The parent can ask the child how she feels about this arrangement or what she thinks might help her to come home on time. And if the child chooses to arrive late, the parent can then follow through with the agreed-upon consequence with love, dignity, and firmness — and without anger and yelling. This kind of discipline teaches children the skills of personal accountability so important for success in today's world.

It's important to involve children as much as possible in the process of setting up consequences. After all, they're much more strongly motivated to obey a rule when they've had a voice in making it.

Children can often come up with creative solutions to problems when given the opportunity, and their ideas on effective consequences may include things that matter to them — things you might never have thought of.

Remember, too, to pay attention to that time-honored maxim of parents everywhere when you're deciding on consequences: "Say what you mean, and mean what you say." Don't tell your whining five-year-old that if she's not in the car this minute, you'll leave for grandma's house without her. She knows as well as you do that grandma lives in the next state and you're not about to leave her standing in the driveway alone. Such empty threats teach children that they only need to listen to about half of what their parents say — not a good way to build trust. Be sure that you're willing and able to follow through *before* you decide on a consequence. (The opposite applies, too: if you've made a promise to your children, do your best to keep it!)

Consequences at Work

Bill had told his kids many times that it was their responsibility to pick up their toys. One day, when he had straightened up the family room for the third time in an afternoon, he sat them down and told them that from now on if they didn't pick up their toys, he would — and the toys would go right onto a shelf and be given to Goodwill in a week. "Do you understand?" he asked his startled children. He explained the new rule and made sure everyone was in agreement. But Bill was realistic. He expected some problems — and they showed up right on schedule.

The first week he was annoyed to see how many things the kids left lying around. Obviously, they didn't believe their dad would do what he'd said — and they didn't particularly care if the toys went to Goodwill. Bill was wise enough to know that his children's lack of concern was his problem, not theirs; apparently he'd given them too many toys that they didn't appreciate. He made a decision not to buy any more toys for his children unless they wanted them enough to save their money and contribute to the purchase.

Bill decided to put the toys on a shelf for a week because everyone makes mistakes. If the kids felt bad about losing a toy he'd picked up, he would say, "Show me you can take care of your toys for a week, and I'll let you try again with the toy you want to keep." Still, the "Goodwill shelf" filled up fast. It was, the family accidentally discovered, a marvelous way of cleaning out unwanted and outgrown toys!

After a while, all that remained were toys the children used and wanted to keep. When these were left lying around, all Bill had to say was, "Do you want to pick your toys up or do you want me to do it?" By now the kids realized that their dad would stick to the logical consequence and give the toys away if they didn't pick them up, so they would scramble to take care of the things they wanted. And did Bill actually take toys his children wanted to Goodwill? Only once — which was enough to teach his children the consequence of choosing not to pick them up.

Was Bill a "mean" father? No. He was a responsible father who used a logical consequence for something that he'd discussed with his kids in advance. Children can learn personal accountability from logical consequences only if parents avoid three traps:

Traps That Defeat Positive Effects of Logical Consequences

1. Using consequences that are not *related*, *respectful*, and *reasonable*.

2. Not having children help decide on logical consequences in advance, or at least letting them know in advance what the logical consequence will be.

3. Not being *kind* and *firm* while enforcing consequences. (This trap underscores the importance of being respectful and reasonable.)

Many parents love the idea of giving up punishment and using logical consequences. However, there are two things to keep in mind when using them.

There's a fine line between logical consequences and punishment. Many parents use punishment in the name of logical consequences, but the disguise is not a good one and children know the difference. They will be discouraged by punishment, no matter what it's called. Only if parents use true logical consequences will children be empowered to accept the personal accountability that fosters self-esteem.

Sometimes parents think logical consequences are the solution to every problem. Not so! We propose many nonpunitive discipline methods throughout this book. Our favorite is family meetings (see Chapter 8), in which everyone in the family works together to brainstorm logical consequences and work on solutions to problems. Another favorite is follow-through.

Follow-Through

Follow-through may seem similar to logical consequences. The important difference is that logical consequences allow children to experience the results of their choices. Follow-through requires that parents decide what *they* will or won't do in response to a child's choices. Follow-through is appropriate only when a parent is present to carry out his or her decision.

When children are young, follow-through is simple. When you say something, mean it. When you mean it, follow through with kindness and firmness. Or, as Rudolf Dreikurs used to say, "Shut your mouth and act." To demonstrate the use of follow-through with young children, we'll describe two scenes. Scene I describes a mother using typical punitive discipline. Scene II portrays another mother using follow-though in response to the same behavior.

SCENE I: It's bedtime. Five-year-old Jennifer is sitting on the floor coloring. Her mother cheerfully says, "It's time to put your crayons away now, honey, and get ready for bed."

Jennifer keeps coloring. Mom's voice gets a little tight. "Did you hear me, Jennifer? It's time to get ready for bed. Put your crayons away."

Jennifer keeps coloring. In a very tight voice Mom says, "Jennifer! I'm going to count to three. If you haven't started putting your crayons away, you're going to get a spanking."

Jennifer keeps coloring. Mom starts to count. When she reaches three, she starts toward Jennifer. Jennifer scrambles to pick up her crayons. Mom spanks her anyway and drags her to her room. Jennifer cries. Mom pours a little salt on the wound by saying, "It serves you right. Why don't you listen to me when I tell you to do something? You can just go to bed without a story now."

Jennifer gets into bed and screams for 15 minutes before falling asleep. Mom says a prayer for retroactive birth control.

SCENE II: It's bedtime. Five-year-old Becky is sitting on the floor coloring. Her mother cheerfully says, "It's time to put your crayons away now, honey, and get ready for bed."

Becky keeps coloring. Mom quietly walks over to Becky, reaches down and takes her hand. Becky tries to pull her hand away and says, "Let me just finish this page."

Mom does not say a word. She gives Becky a kind but knowing glance, and firmly but gently pulls her up from the floor. Becky starts to complain. Mom says, "Do you want to pick out your bedtime story or do you want me to?"

Becky says in a pouting voice, "I want to."

Mom says, "Fine. Call me as soon as you're ready for bed and I'll come and read as much as I can before eight o'clock. The longer you take to get ready for bed, the less time we'll have for reading."

Becky knows Mom means what she says, so she gets ready as fast as she can. When Mom finishes reading she tells Becky, "You didn't pick the crayons up tonight. In the morning you can pick them up before kindergarten or I will pick them up and put them on the high shelf."

If Becky doesn't pick up the crayons, Mom will follow through on what she said. Becky and her mom have already agreed that when any toys go on the high shelf, Becky must demonstrate that she's ready to get them back by picking up her toys responsibly for at least two days.

Follow-through is more effective with older kids when they're involved in some preliminary preparation. As soon as they're old enough to be involved in decision making, we suggest the following four steps:

Four Steps for Effective Follow-Through

1. Have a friendly discussion during which everyone gets to voice his or her feelings and thoughts about the issue.

2. Brainstorm for possible solutions and choose one on which both adult and child agree.

3. Agree on a specific time deadline (to the minute).
4. Simply follow through by holding the child responsible for keeping the agreement.

The following example shows how one father moved from punishment, which had never produced satisfactory results, to follow-through, which got the job done and greatly improved his relationship with his daughter.

Fifteen-year-old Karen had accepted the job of keeping the kitchen clean. She rarely did it unless Jim, her dad, scolded and threatened to ground her for a week if it wasn't done.

After one particularly heated argument, Jim realized that his method wasn't working too well and decided to try follow-through. He asked Karen if she would be willing to work with him on a solution so they could end their power struggle over the kitchen. Karen agreed reluctantly — she was expecting a lecture and wasn't sure what this new approach might mean. She was surprised when her dad said sincerely, "Karen, I'd really like to hear what's going on for you regarding the kitchen. Do you think it's too big a job for you, or unfair, or are you too busy?"

Karen fidgeted and said, "No, Dad. I know I should do it. I always mean to. I just get busy and forget."

Jim said, "I have a hunch that something else might be involved, too. I've been pretty bossy about telling you what to do, and very insulting to you when you don't jump to obey my commands on schedule. Could it be that you're showing me that I can't make you if you don't want to?"

Karen grinned sheepishly. Jim laughed and said, "I thought so. I remember feeling the same way, and I don't blame you. In fact, when I think about it, I have to admire your spunk in refusing to be treated that way. I really want to stop being bossy and insulting. Are you willing to work with me on ways to treat each other respectfully?"

Karen said, "Sounds good to me, Dad."

Jim paused for a moment. "How about brainstorming with me on some solutions to the kitchen problem? I have one suggestion. We could both get extra jobs so we could earn enough money to hire a maid."

Karen laughed and said, "We could just let it go and eat pizza every night."

Jim added, "We could try and con your friends into doing it."

Karen was quiet for a moment. "Or I could just do it. I know I agreed to, and I don't do much else to help."

Jim said, "Well, that's the solution I'd prefer, if you're really willing and don't feel forced to by a bossy dad. Would you be willing to agree to a specific time deadline for when it will be done? Then I won't say a word unless it's not done by the deadline."

Karen said, "How about Sunday night?"

Jim shook his head and smiled. "I could enjoy the weekend a lot more if the kitchen was clean before Saturday."

Karen sighed. "Okay, I'll do it by Friday."

Jim asked, "What time Friday?"

"Da-ad! I'll do it by Friday."

"It will be easier for me to keep my mouth shut and not nag if the deadline is very specific."

"Okay, okay. How about six o'clock Friday evening?"

"Sounds good to me, kiddo."

It's now 6:00 p.m. the following Friday. The kitchen is a maze of dirty dishes and leftover food, and Karen is chatting happily on the phone. Jim is not surprised; he expected this. He's ready to follow through.

When Karen hangs up the phone, Jim places his hand on her shoulder and says, "Karen, it's six o'clock and the kitchen is not cleaned."

Karen says, "Aw, Dad, I had to talk to Shannon about homework. I'll do it later."

Jim says simply, "What was our agreement?"

Karen squirms and there's a hint of irritation in her voice. "Come on, Dad. Don't be uptight. I'll do it right after I call Shannon back."

Jim simply smiles, gives his daughter a knowing grin, and points to his watch. Karen's lower lip juts out. "Okay, okay. I'm going. Talk about uptight!"

Jim manages to ignore both the insult and Karen's obvious annoyance. He says, "Thanks, Karen. I really appreciate your willingness to keep your agreement."

Some parents say, "My son or daughter wouldn't give in that easily." We disagree. When we follow the Four Steps to Effective Follow-Through and avoid the following Four Traps That Defeat Effective Follow-Through, kids do cooperate, even when they don't especially want to.

Four Traps That Defeat Effective Follow-Through

1. Wanting kids to have the same priorities as adults.

2. Judging and criticizing instead of sticking to the issue.

3. Not getting agreements (noncoerced) in advance that include a specific time deadline. (This step is not necessary for children too young to make an agreement.)

4. Not maintaining dignity and respect for the child and for yourself.

If you reread the example of Karen and her father, you'll see that Jim didn't expect Karen to be excited about cleaning the kitchen. When Jim thought about it, he could name many things that were higher priorities for Karen—things like zits, how to pay for a car when she gets her license, getting a job to pay for insurance and gas, how much homework to do without being called a nerd, what to do about drugs, sex, and college, worrying about whether she'll have a date, wondering what her friends think of her. Cleaning the kitchen wasn't even in the top 100. However, it's still important for Karen to contribute to the family in meaningful ways.

Notice that Jim avoided judgments and criticism and stuck to the issue of the agreement. The more Karen talked, the less her dad had to say. He simply gave her a knowing grin and pointed to his watch. This was effective because Karen knew she had agreed to the deadline. Jim maintained dignity and respect both for his daughter and for himself throughout the follow-through process.

Some people object to follow-through. They say, "We don't want to have to remind our kids to keep their agreements. We expect them to be responsible without any reminders from us."

We have three questions for these people. Have you noticed how responsible your kids are about keeping agreements that are important to them? Do you think cleaning the kitchen or mowing the lawn is really important to them? When you don't take time to remind them with dignity and respect, do you spend time scolding, lecturing, and punishing them for not keeping their agreements? Even if it's not important to them, it's important to have them do it anyway, to teach them responsibility, mutual respect, and shared contribution. Follow-through takes less energy and is much more loving—and productive—than scolding, lecturing, and punishing.

Adults are not using their common sense when they expect kids to use their free will to follow adult priorities. Young people are very good at using their free will to follow their own priorities! Follow-through is a respectful way of helping kids live up to appropriate adult expectations.

Once we understand that kids have their own priorities but still need to follow some of *our* priorities, follow-through can make parenting pleasurable, magical, and fun. We can see the things kids do as cute, adorable, and normal instead of lazy, inconsiderate, and irresponsible.

Follow-through helps parents to be proactive and thoughtful instead of reactive and inconsiderate. Follow-through helps us to empower kids by respecting who they are while teaching them the importance of making a contribution to the family. In the following example, Mrs. Ruiz offers a different slant on follow-through:

Mrs. Ruiz had tried nagging her 17-year-old daughter, Nita, about the cereal bowls the girl left in her room. She would find as many as seven bowls in Nita's room, coated with hardened cereal that made them very difficult to wash. And it wasn't unusual for the rest of the family to have to search high and low for a clean bowl when they needed one.

One day, when Mrs. Ruiz was scolding Nita for being so inconsiderate, Nita said, "I'm sorry, Mom. It's just that I'm so busy with school, my job, homework, and dance lessons. I need some time for my friends and some fun. I just keep forgetting about the bowls."

Mrs. Ruiz suddenly realized the truth of what Nita was saying. Nita was an extremely busy teenager with a lot of pressure in her life. Her mom remembered all the little errands Nita did for her, her generally cheerful attitude, and her responsibility in balancing all the demands on her time.

Mrs. Ruiz said, "Honey, you're right. You do have a lot going on in your life, and you're doing a darn good job keeping up with it all. I'm really very proud of you. I'm going to quit nagging you about these silly bowls. I'll tell you what—when I notice them, I'll just take them to the kitchen and put them in water to soak for a while. It would make me feel good to do that for you as a reminder to both of us about how much I love you."

Nita looked at her mom with genuine surprise and gratitude. "Gee, thanks, Mom. I'll try harder, but I really do appreciate your understanding and support."

Mrs. Ruiz felt so much better. It was much easier just to pick up the bowls than to nag and get upset about it.

In other circumstances it might be inappropriate for Mrs. Ruiz to do too much for her daughter. However, in this case Nita was not taking advantage. She was being a very responsible teenager in most areas of her life.

Using natural and logical consequences and follow-through are two excellent alternatives to punitive discipline or permissiveness. These nonpunitive methods help change behavior while maintaining dignity and respect for all concerned.

Consequences and follow-through are two ways to help children learn the life skills they need to feel good about themselves while teaching them to be contributing members of society through personal accountability.

The next chapter continues the theme of nonpunitive parenting by getting children involved as a family team.

CHAPTER 8

Making Your Family a Team

There's no doubt that single parenthood can be challenging for everyone concerned, and that too often we and our children arrive at being a single-parent family laden with heavy emotional baggage. But, as we've seen, life for single parents and their children can hold some wonderful possibilities as well.

Drawing Children into the Circle

If what human beings really need is to belong and to feel significant, worthwhile, and needed, then a single-parent family can provide tremendous opportunities for young people to fulfill those needs. Single parents rarely have to manufacture things for their children to do; they can say with absolute honesty, "It really makes my life easier when you help me and I really appreciate you. Thanks!" And that can make a child feel truly important.

There's sometimes a temptation to make children *too* important, to cast them in the role of the missing spouse. A son can become the new "man of the family"; a daughter can become Mom's best friend and confidante or Dad's "little homemaker." It's natural for a single parent to want someone to lean on, someone to share the responsibilities of keeping this new kind of family together. But children are still children, and the weight of being the "little man" or the "little woman" can be far too heavy for their young shoulders.

Occasionally parents go to the opposite extreme, taking on themselves all of the responsibility for chores, school work, and decisions. Their children, they may believe, have suffered enough by losing the active involvement of one parent in their home and shouldn't be expected to work or be responsible as well.

Neither approach works well in the long run. As we've mentioned, overly responsible children can become their parent's caretakers, bearing unnecessary emotional burdens, while children who aren't involved in family work at all may begin to simply slide through life, expecting others always to make decisions for them — and to clean up after them.

Perhaps a more constructive idea is to approach life in a single-parent family as a cooperative effort. "We're a team," a parent might say to his children, "and this family needs each one of us to work." Children want to make a contribution; a parent needs to know that her children are learning to handle life for themselves. Family life, even in a single-parent family, is a circle, and when each member is carrying just the right amount of weight it rolls along smoothly.

Family Work: Opportunity or Oppression?

Family work — those tasks that need to be done to keep a home running smoothly and peacefully — can be either an accepted part of life in a family or an endless hassle. It's probably best not to define these tasks as "chores," things you do because you have to, things you'll be nagged or penalized for not doing. Family work means cooperation, making a contribution that helps the entire family. Believe it or not, most children react with enthusiasm when they're given opportunities to be valued contributors to their family. Being part of the team, especially when it's approached with love, humor, and respect, can be a wonderfully empowering and encouraging experience for parent and child alike.

Every member of a family, from the youngest to the oldest, can do something worthwhile. A three-year-old can put napkins at each place at the table; older children can clear away and wash dishes, take out trash, or water plants; teens can help out in a variety of ways. Too often, though, what parents notice (and nag about) is what *didn't* get done. Or they set their standards and expectations too high and provide little or no "on-the-job training." Family work can then become a discouraging experience to young people—and getting them to participate turns into a major problem. When parents take the time not only to notice what *did* get done but to teach, encourage, appreciate, and give positive feedback, the entire process can actually become an enjoyable part of family life.

It's easy to view children as weighty responsibilities, or as lesser beings who often get in our way. Actually, children are remarkable resources. They are—or can be, when given the chance—creative, energetic and ingenious. How can single parents tap into that energy and creativity? And how can we make life in our family like a well-balanced circle, embracing everyone and rolling along smoothly?

The Family Meeting

One important way of creating a spirit of teamwork and cooperation is the family meeting. It doesn't matter whether your family consists of one parent and one child or one parent and several children—you're a family, and family meetings will strengthen your family team.

Family meetings may be a new idea to you. You may wonder what their benefits are and how you go about holding them. You may also wonder where on earth you'll find the time for one more thing. There are many excuses for not having family meetings: "With all I have to juggle, how can I find time for family meetings?" "There are only two of us and we solve problems while driving in the car." "My kids are so good we don't need to have family meetings." All of these excuses ignore the long-range benefits of family meetings.

Long-Range Benefits of Family Meetings

1. Setting aside time to gather as a family demonstrates a commitment to the family. Often we keep appointments with co-workers, friends, even strangers, but not with our children.

2. Family meetings are an opportunity to create mutual respect through joint problem solving and to make time for conversation, understanding, and staying in tune with one another.

3. Family meetings give children the chance to feel that their thoughts, feelings, and ideas are listened to and taken seriously (and parents may gain ideas and insights they didn't have before). What better way to build self-esteem, confidence, and feelings of capability?

4. In our busy, stressful lives, time for relaxed meals together and long conversations afterward can be difficult to find. A tradition of family meetings can become the foundation for wonderful times together and special memories for the future.

How Do You "Do" Family Meetings?

Just as families come in different shapes, sizes, and flavors, family meetings will differ in their priorities and their details. There are a few important points to keep in mind, though.

1. Family meetings should be a priority. Most families find that setting aside a certain time each week works best. This may be an evening when no one has activities to dash off to, or a meal when everyone is present. Try not to make other plans for that time and don't allow yourself to be interrupted by the phone or other distractions. Let your children know that you consider this time with them a very important part of your week.

2. Begin each meeting with compliments and appreciations. Look for—and comment on—the positive things each member of your family has done, and teach your children to do the same. This can feel awkward, especially for siblings who are more accustomed to put-downs, arguments, and hassles. But the feelings of worth and significance that result will be worth the effort—and your entire meeting will be off to an encouraging start.

3. Keep an "agenda board" in a handy place (the refrigerator seems to be a favorite) and encourage members of the family to write down ideas and problems during the week for consideration at the next meeting—and then be sure to discuss each item. Sometimes having a place to vent their frustration is all kids really need, and by the time the meeting rolls around the problem has been solved—or forgotten. At other times the family will need to brainstorm for ideas to solve the problems.

4. Problem-solving and planning activities should respect the rights and opinions of each member of the family. During brainstorming, all ideas, no matter how unworkable they may appear at first, should be accepted respectfully. All it takes is one "Well, *that's* a stupid idea!" to sour a child on family meetings for good. Once everyone has had a chance to brainstorm ideas, you can proceed with figuring out which ideas will work and

why, and everyone can agree on the best plan. In this way brainstorming becomes a learning experience, and an opportunity to teach your children valuable problem-solving skills.

5. Decisions should be made by consensus rather than by a majority vote. Voting only builds resentment in those who "lost." If your family can't agree on something, put it off until the next meeting. By then, everyone will have cooled off and may have had time to come up with new ideas.

6. Have a chairperson and a secretary to record decisions, and rotate these positions. Children love to be in charge and can do a good job once they understand the procedure. This also demonstrates that the parent is willing to listen to and consider the thoughts and abilities of each child.

7. End each family meeting with plans for a family activity in the coming week, or with a game or a favorite dessert.

But Does It Really Work?

It was a busy morning—as usual—at the Taylor home. Marlene was preparing for her day at work and trying to see that her three daughters had some breakfast before they left for school. She was sipping a cup of coffee when a long wail from down the hall caught her attention.

Mandy, her 14-year-old, stormed out of her room with a crumpled blouse in one hand. "Mo-om!" she howled. "I wanted to wear my favorite blouse to school today but Kim wore it and got it all dirty—and she didn't even ask me first."

Kim, 13, was not far behind. "Well, Mandy took my best jeans," she sulked. "And Trish keeps taking my hair stuff."

"Did not!" came eight-year-old Trish's voice from the bathroom.

Marlene closed her eyes for a moment and took a deep breath. "Sounds to me like you're all feeling frustrated with the borrowing that's going on," she said. "Have you written it down on the agenda for our next family meeting?"

The three girls looked at each other and shook their heads. Marlene sighed, then smiled. "Well, why don't you write it down?" she said. "Our next meeting is Thursday night and we can work on the problem then. Now it's time for school — you'd better finish getting dressed."

Thursday evening rolled around and Marlene gathered her daughters around the cleared kitchen table. "Kim," she said, "it's your turn to be chairperson. And, Mandy, you're secretary."

"OK," Kim began. "I want Mandy to quit taking my stuff."

"Whoa," her mom said. "How do we begin our family meetings?"

There was a stubborn silence. The girls were still angry and found appreciating each other a tricky task. Finally Kim said, only a little sullenly, "I appreciate that Mandy helped me with my math homework the other night." That broke the ice. Other compliments and a funny story followed, and before too long the family was ready to begin problem solving.

Kim took charge. "The agenda says we need to talk about borrowing each other's things. Does anyone have any ideas?"

It didn't take long to brainstorm quite a list. The girls decided that Mandy and Kim, who shared a bedroom, should have separate drawers and racks for their things. The owner's name could be written on each item's label with a laundry pen. Each girl agreed to ask her sisters *before* she borrowed something and to make sure it was returned clean, pressed, and ready to wear.

The girls agreed that baskets on the bathroom counter would help them keep their hair supplies separate. Mandy and Kim, who were almost the same size and were most likely to borrow each other's clothing, agreed that taking something without permission or returning it dirty (or not at all) would give the other sister the right to wear the article of her choice for a day—and to return it without laundering it.

Marlene looked at the list of solutions Mandy had written down. "Are you all willing to try this for a week?" she asked. The girls nodded their heads. "We can check at our next meeting to see how it's going, but if you're happy with this, it's fine with me. Now, what shall we do this weekend?"

"Go shopping for more clothes!" exclaimed Trish, and they all laughed together.

Family meetings aren't the solution to every problem. But they do provide a time and a place for members of a family to listen to each other's thoughts, ideas, grievances, and accomplishments, and to learn to work together to find mutually acceptable ways out of the dilemmas and controversies of everyday life.

Remember, too, that your "family" can include just about anyone. And family meetings often work best when they include all of the people who are directly involved, such as babysitters, close friends, or even teachers.

For example, Phyllis was a single mother with one six-year-old son, Matthew. Matthew was a bright child—a little too bright for his own good. He was creative and verbal, and usually had no trouble getting around people. Phyllis had recently started a new business and found herself needing to work long hours, but she worried about child care for her son. The solution presented itself in the form of an older woman who was willing to live in. Phyllis drove off to work whistling the first morning the sitter moved in—and arrived home late that night to find total disaster.

Matthew, it turned out, had used all of his intelligence to manipulate his new sitter, knowing Mom wasn't around to enforce the rules. He was still up when Phyllis came home, although it was a school night. He had been out playing in the neighborhood until 7:30 p.m., and threw a tantrum when the sitter managed to make him come inside then—even though he knew Mom expected him to come in at 5:00. Phyllis scolded and punished, but the situation was hopeless; eventually the sitter gave up in despair, and Phyllis went back to the hassle of trying to make other arrangements with neighborhood sitters, and to work fewer hours.

A few months later, as Phyllis found her business thriving and demanding more of her time, she decided to try a live-in sitter again. But this time Phyllis decided to include the sitter in family meetings. The sitter, Aggie, was intrigued with the idea. They involved Matthew in looking at all of the possible problems and making all of the rules — and they found that Matthew enjoyed putting his creativity to constructive uses. Because Matthew was involved in creating the rules, he was more inclined to obey them.

Life ran much more smoothly, although it was far from perfect; still, when there was a problem, Phyllis, Aggie, or Matthew would put it on the agenda and they would work on solutions at their next meeting. Phyllis was thrilled, Aggie remained sane, and Matthew learned that being part of the solution was better than being part of the problem — well, most of the time. Five weeks later Phyllis shared with her parenting group that she couldn't believe how smoothly things were going. She told them things were almost perfect, and wished she'd known about family meetings sooner.

Making Changes as a Family

It's tempting to use family meetings only for solving problems and deciding on consequences — after all, they work so well for that purpose. But gathering as a family in a comfortable and predictable way is also a wonderful means to share information, to find out how everyone is feeling, to stay in touch, and to deal *together* with change.

When Brian sat down with his two children for their weekly family meeting, he was a bit apprehensive — he had some news to share and he wasn't at all sure how his kids would react.

As Brian placed a big bowl of popcorn in the center of the table (and took a large handful himself), he asked Kate, his 14-year-old daughter, to start with some compliments.

Kate and nine-year-old Robby talked warmly for a few minutes about their week. Robby had been selected "most valuable player" at his Little League game, and his grin brightened the whole room. Kate had successfully resolved a big argument with a friend at school, and thanked her little brother for feeding Muffin, the dog, so she could go to the movies with a friend. As the conversation slowed, both kids turned to their father.

"You're not saying much, Dad," Kate said. "What's been going on for you?"

"Well," Brian said slowly, "I got a big promotion at work."

"All *right!*" Robby exclaimed. "Will you make more money? Can we go to Disneyland this summer?"

"That's cool, Dad," Kate chimed in with a smile.

"Yeah, it's cool," Brian said. "I'll make more money, Rob, which should make life a little easier—although I don't know about Disneyland. But there's one catch. You see, the new job is in Florida."

There was a long silence while Kate and Robby digested this information. "Will we be able to get a new house?" Robby asked hopefully. "Maybe one with a swimming pool?"

Brian smiled. "Katie, you're pretty quiet. What's going on for you?"

When Kate looked up at her father, there was an unmistakable quiver in her lower lip. "But Dad, I'll have to leave my school and my friends, and I was just picked to be on the drill team. What about that? And what about Muffin?" And then the big question. "What about Mom? Does she know?"

Brian explained to his children that their mother knew and approved of the move. Kate and Robby would visit her just as they always had, but they would fly in from Florida instead of taking the short bus ride they had now. It seemed, though, that each time Brian answered a question, ten new ones popped up in its place. "Wait a moment," Brian finally said. "Let's write all of this down."

On a large sheet of paper, Brian listed the family's concerns. His children were worried about making new friends, helping to pick a new place to live, packing all of their belongings, finding a new church, being the new kids in school, even moving the dog.

When the family had listed as many concerns as they could think of, Brian listed possible solutions next to each one. Brian would be visiting Florida in a couple of weeks, and he agreed to take pictures of possible homes and schools so the kids could help him pick one. The family agreed that they should have a going-away party, and that Kate and Robby could each pack one box with their most important belongings to take in the car, so they wouldn't have to wait for the moving van. And Brian agreed that they could return, possibly at Christmas, to visit their old home and friends.

"So how are you really feeling?" Brian finally asked.

"Sad," Kate replied. "I'm happy for you, Daddy, but I can't help being sad about leaving."

"I know, honey. What about you, Rob?"

"I'm kinda excited," Rob said thoughtfully. "I mean, isn't Disney World in Florida?"

Even Kate couldn't help giggling. "You know, kids," Brian said, "we'll always be a family, no matter where we go. And I know that with you two to help me, we'll make our new house a real home in no time. It may take time, but you'll make great friends—after all, who could resist such fantastic kids?" And Brian gave each of his children an extra-tight hug.

Family meetings won't magically make problems go away and they do take time and effort, but they're a wonderful way for single parents and their children to build a new identity as a family, to learn to appreciate each other, and to discover that single-parent homes aren't "broken" homes, but work quite well indeed!

The Problem of Enmeshment

Love, trust, and closeness are important elements in making a single-parent family work, but sometimes the members of a single-parent family "team" can get a little too close.

Nancy, a single mom, had been alone for almost three years and Stephanie, her five-year-old daughter, was the center of her life. In fact, since Stephanie's father had moved out, Nancy had never spent a night away from her daughter. Because Nancy was disabled and didn't work outside the home, her days with Stephanie had been a succession of picnics, trips to the park, tea parties, and other shared activities.

However, change was looming on Nancy's horizon. Stephanie was ready to begin kindergarten and her mother found the thought of entire days without her daughter unbearable. In addition, she realized that Stephanie would begin to make new friends and develop new interests, and Nancy began to be afraid that somehow she wouldn't be as important in her daughter's life.

"Perhaps," she thought to herself, "I could school Stephanie at home." The more she thought about it, the more she liked the idea of keeping Stephanie with her and shielding her from the difficulties and influences of the outside world.

Nancy was wise enough, though, to realize that she needed some help in making such a big decision. There was free counseling available through her church, and though it was hard to leave Stephanie with a sitter even for an hour or two, Nancy made an appointment to discuss her situation with a counselor.

It wasn't difficult for the counselor to see the causes of Nancy's dilemma. Single parents often focus a huge amount of their time and energy on their children. They may be struggling with the transition from being part of a couple to being single. They may be feeling lonely and afraid. They may be worried about—and trying to compensate for—the effects on their children of growing up in a single-parent family. And because they love their children, they sometimes become over-involved in their lives, blurring the healthy parent-child boundaries, and becoming enmeshed.

When this happens, it's difficult for a single parent to let children grow up and develop relationships outside the family —or for the parent to develop a life of his or her own. Children may eventually feel trapped or overwhelmed, and when they try to break free, the parent feels hurt and betrayed.

Nancy's counselor understood the deep love and the strong bond between mother and daughter. But she suggested to Nancy that letting go of Stephanie a little at a time was a healthy and loving thing to do. Stephanie needed to have friends her own age; she needed to learn how to get along in the world and to have all the experiences and adventures that school would bring. Nancy could share in all of that without needing to restrict it.

Just as important, the counselor added, Nancy needed to begin a new life of her own. Joining a single parents' group would be a beginning; taking a class, or going out for dinner or a movie with a friend, would be a good step as well.

Nancy knew in her heart that the counselor had given her good advice. She knew she and Stephanie would be healthier if they learned to spend time away from each other. What surprised Nancy was how hard it was for Stephanie to make the break. The first time Nancy hired a babysitter so she could go to a movie with a friend, Stephanie cried and clung to her mother as she tried to leave. Nancy was tempted to give in and stay home, but instead she peeled Stephanie off of her body, said "Honey, I'll be home in three hours," and left. Nancy didn't have a good time with her friend, and didn't remember one scene from the movie. But when she got home, Stephanie was happily playing a game with the babysitter.

"She quit crying as soon as you drove away," the sitter reported, "and we've had a great evening." Nancy quickly realized that the next time she went out it would be easier— both for her and for her daughter.

It took a while for Nancy to face her fears of losing Stephanie, and for Stephanie to face her fears of losing her mother. Both had to develop the courage to let each other have some independence. Gradually, though, Nancy discovered that both she and Stephanie were happier as they developed new friendships and interests — and they enjoyed even more the time that they spent together.

A healthy single-parent family can be a wonderful place to grow up, but making the necessary adjustments can take time and courage. Building a sense of closeness, of being a *team*, takes time, and sometimes some healing is necessary first for the parent and the children. The result, though, is worth the effort: contented, healthy children; contented, healthy parents; and a home that is comfortable, safe, and welcoming for everyone.

CHAPTER 9

Redefining Yourself as a Single Parent

The first months, even years, of single parenthood can be a busy time. Eventually, though, the dust settles a bit and life relaxes into a routine. And at some point a single parent may begin to say, "But what about me? Don't I have needs too?"

Sometimes being a single parent seems to be all about the *parent* part. Our children are our major priority — providing for them, helping them grow and flourish, keeping their lives on an even keel. What we sometimes fail to realize is that to be healthy, effective parents, we must first be healthy, effective human beings — and that can feel like a tall order. "Where," you may wonder, "do I find the time and energy to 'get a life'?"

Social life often seems to revolve around couples. When you're not part of one it's easy to feel lonely, different, set apart. If you've been married for a long time, it may be difficult to adjust to being on your own; much of your identity can be tied to your spouse and your old way of life. Hitting the singles scene may seem far too intimidating.

Single parents also may find themselves with jobs and roles they never anticipated. Figuring out the income tax may terrify a single mother whose ex-husband always did that, while dealing with a daughter's clothing and hair styling may baffle a single dad. Lifestyles may have changed dramatically. Adults who never really worried about money may suddenly find themselves scrambling to get by, unable to enjoy activities and pleasures they took for granted before. And all single parents inevitably find themselves longing for just a little free time, independence, and adult conversation.

Can you meet the demands of single parenthood, do all the jobs required of you, and still find time for a healthy adult life? Not only can you—you must! Taking care of yourself is one of the most important jobs you have.

Taking care of yourself can take many different forms. For Carolyn, it meant making some sweeping and traumatic changes in her life. Carolyn had been married for 15 years and had two beautiful children, Paul and Cheryl. During Carolyn's marriage, her husband had made all of the decisions about finances and business. Steve was a good husband and a kind man, but there was never any doubt about who was in control. Other than working very hard in her home and in the PTA during her children's school years, Carolyn had never held a job during her marriage.

The day arrived when Carolyn realized she'd lost *herself* in her marriage. She was her husband's wife and her children's mother, but she wasn't sure *Carolyn* even existed. She suddenly knew that the old identities were no longer enough for her. She felt stifled. Paul and Cheryl were now entering their teens and were busy with their friends and school activities; Steve was busy with work and seemed uninterested in Carolyn—except to find out what she was cooking for dinner.

Carolyn suggested counseling to Steve, who wasn't interested. She tried hobbies and clubs. Nothing seemed to make any difference. She decided that she had to take charge of her own life. When she announced to her husband that she wanted a divorce, he retorted, "If you want a divorce, you're the one who will have to move out." He believed she would never leave. Carolyn surprised him and herself by taking some of their savings, finding a small apartment, and moving out.

Carolyn hadn't worked in 15 years. She had only a high school education. She hadn't gone to college or developed any marketable skills, and she knew she couldn't make a living organizing school bake sales, carnivals, and other activities. It was a terrifying experience for her, but the sense of opportunity and freedom was heady and she was determined to make her life better.

The first year was the most difficult. At times her fear was so great that she felt completely defeated. Sometimes she was tempted to return to her old life. But she kept remembering her restlessness before her divorce and her determination to take care of herself. She knew she couldn't go back. She found a job in a department store, and by working twice as hard as anyone else she earned a promotion to department manager. After two years, her divorce was final and her children chose to come and live with her.

Carolyn never looked back. She did her best to help Paul and Cheryl adjust, accepting their anger and hurt (and, later, their support) with understanding. Although she experienced both grief and guilt, she worked through those emotions. They began to empower her rather than to deplete her.

Steve, on the other hand, was so full of anger and resentment at Carolyn that he spent thousands of dollars fighting both the divorce and the custody agreement. He was devastated when his children chose to live with their mother instead of with him. Long after Carolyn had begun to thrive in her new life, Steve continued to wallow in bitterness.

Are sweeping changes—such as divorce—always necessary to teach us to take care of ourselves? No, of course not. But change can be a catalyst to help us develop new courage and creativity. We always have opportunities to turn negative experiences into positive ones. But if we are to be creative, we must be willing to take care of ourselves—an important ingredient of self-esteem.

Self-Esteem? What Self-Esteem?

Self-esteem is the picture we have of ourselves, the sum of the decisions we've made about who we are, what we're capable of, what others think of us, and whether we're "good enough." Everyone has self-esteem, but not everyone's self-esteem is healthy. Sometimes the events and circumstances that make us single parents also leave gaping wounds in our opinion of ourselves.

Single parents may be struggling with feelings of rejection and hurt because a partner has left them, or they may be feeling guilty because they chose to leave. A single parent may feel anxious, incapable of raising whole, healthy children, and all too aware of the mistakes he or she has made in the past. Everyone is occasionally haunted by feelings of inadequacy and failure, but single parents sometimes find that those feelings are constant companions. The result can be a sense of hopelessness, lack of confidence, and deep discouragement. Allowing those attitudes to take root in your heart will affect the way you approach your life, the way you behave, what you accomplish — or even whether you attempt anything at all.

Children too can suffer in the aftermath of a death, divorce, or perceived abandonment. Because their world is centered on themselves and their own perceptions, children often believe that their parents' problems are the result of something they said, or did, or wished — no matter how many times we tell them differently. A child's thinking is often "magical." If a child was angry at Mom and Mom suddenly disappeared from his life, it *must* have been his fault. Children who sense tension between their parents often increase their misbehavior in an attempt to keep their parents busy and involved with them — and, in the process, to keep them together. "Failure" in the form of death or divorce is devastating, and children usually blame themselves for it. Rebuilding your children's self-esteem and sense of worth may seem like a huge task when your own is heavily damaged. How do we go about healing self-esteem? Where do we begin?

Healing Your Self-Esteem

"Maybe some people can heal," you may be saying, "but I can't help the way I feel." It may come as a revelation to learn that feelings can be changed (and it may seem far easier to stay stuck where you are), but it's important that you begin to examine your beliefs and attitudes about yourself and to change the ones that are keeping you from healing and growing. Remember that your children will adopt many of your beliefs; fear, guilt, and depression, while natural and unavoidable for a while, will affect your entire family.

Everyone agrees that it's critical for children to have a healthy sense of self-esteem: believing in themselves and in their intrinsic worth is what gives children the courage to try new things, to take risks, and to resist peer pressure. What we need to remember is that much of that sense of worth is learned from parents. Children learn to respect and accept who they are when their parents show them how — by doing it themselves.

The first step in healing your self-esteem is to realize that you're "good enough" just the way you are. That doesn't mean there aren't areas you'd like to improve — all of us struggle to work through different aspects of our personalities and habits. But you don't have to finish the work (in other words, you don't have to be perfect) to be a lovable and valuable human being.

There are a number of things you can do that will help you not only heal your own self-esteem, but build that of your children. They are each discussed here: (1) learning to separate a person from his/her actions, (2) learning to look for the positive, (3) beginning to affirm yourself, (4) not being afraid to change when it feels right, (5) learning to value the moment, and (6) taking the time to nurture yourself.

Begin with yourself. It takes time and patience, but eventually you *and* your children may find that you're able to pursue life with confidence and hope.

Learn to separate the person from the actions.

The fact that you've made mistakes and messed up doesn't mean you're a bad person. We're usually our own worst critics — we're quick to dismiss ourselves as worthless when we feel we've made wrong choices. But a person's worth is not defined by what he or she does. It rests on who that person is, and all of us deserve dignity and respect. Rudolf Dreikurs spoke often of having "the courage to be imperfect." This means recognizing that all of us — parents and children alike — make mistakes, and that expecting perfection will only lead to disappointment. When you make a mistake, learn to forgive yourself, dust yourself off, and try again. If your children see that mistakes are not fatal and that forgiveness is possible, they'll be more willing to admit their own mistakes and to handle them in a healthy manner. Knowing it's okay to make mistakes eliminates one of the reasons why children sometimes lie, and creates a much more positive atmosphere in your home. After all, doesn't it make more sense to allow everyone to be human?

It's wise to keep in mind that a child who misbehaves is not a "bad" child; he is simply a child who made a wrong choice or a mistake. It's possible to say to that child, "I love you; you're a great kid and I'm glad I have you in my life. But what you just *did* is a real problem. What do you think we can do about it?"

Children have a tendency to believe what their parents say about them. Most of us can remember a time when someone told us we were ugly or stupid, or belittled us in some way. Some of us are still living our lives under the influence of those carelessly cruel words. When we tell a child she's bad, lazy, stupid, or any other negative label, she believes us. Oh, she may argue with us. But a little voice inside tells her that if Mom (who knows everything) says she's stupid, she really must be stupid. And before long, you'll have a discouraged child who no longer tries because she believes success just isn't possible.

Happily, the reverse is also true. Saying good things to our children will encourage them and build them up.

Learn to look for the positive.

We live in a world that focuses on the negative. Any one of us could easily write a list of what we *don't* like about ourselves, our children, our jobs, our lives. We're trained to immediately spot the chore that *didn't* get done or the grade on the report card that *isn't* acceptable, and all too often our conversations with those we love revolve around what's *wrong*.

Learning to spot the positive takes a little more effort, but it can change the way we look at everything — including our- selves. Take a moment soon and write down 10 things you like about yourself. Then make a point of complimenting yourself on those things at least once a day. Most adults find it surpris- ingly hard to find and acknowledge the good things about themselves. We've been taught that liking ourselves is "brag- ging" or "pride" — and we all know that pride goes before a fall. Or we've accepted as truth someone else's opinions about us. We need to dispel these false images and myths. Acknowledging what's good about ourselves is part of seeing ourselves honestly, and it will help carry us through our inevitable mistakes.

It helps to make a list of the things you like about your children, too, and to make a point of commenting on those things. Encouragement is probably the single most powerful tool in building self-esteem — and all too often it's one we forget to use. Take time to notice when your children do what they're supposed to; tell them you appreciate their cooperation, their good behavior, their sharing, their cheerful smiles. Thank them with a smile for the four tasks they completed after school, and wait until later to remind them about the one they forgot. Behavior that is noticed and appreciated is more likely to be repeated. Even more important, your recognition teaches children to value themselves.

Denise was just hanging up the phone when her boss poked his head in the door. "When you have a minute, Denise," he said, "I'd like to see you in my office."

Denise's stomach curled up into a tight little knot. What had she done wrong? Had she forgotten something? Made a mistake? As she walked into her boss's office she expected the worst.

Ken, Denise's boss, waved his hand at an empty chair. "Sit down, Denise — and don't look so worried!" he grinned. "Actually, I've been meaning to talk to you for some time. I've been noticing what a terrific job you do. I know you've been under a lot of pressure at home, yet your attitude here has been wonderful. Our clients love you, the quality of your work is great, and your sense of humor keeps us all going sometimes. I just wanted you to know how much we appreciate everything you do."

Denise realized that her jaw had dropped, and Ken laughed. "We supervisors don't do this sort of thing often enough, do we?" he asked. "Did you think I was going to fire you or something?" When Denise smiled ruefully, Ken continued, "I guess I don't blame you. Somehow it's harder to find time to say good things than it is to criticize. Anyway, keep up the great work."

When Denise opened her own front door that evening and looked around, she had a flash of inspiration. Some chores hadn't been done, she could see, but the kids were playing quietly together and it was obvious they had all done their homework — the books and papers were neatly stacked for her to check.

"Hey, guys," she called out to her children. Three faces turned towards her with apprehensive looks, and she realized they probably felt much as she had when Ken had spoken to her. She smiled as warmly as she could.

"I just wanted you to know how much I enjoy coming home. You look so cozy there together and I can see you've all done your homework. You know, I really appreciate it when you do what you're supposed to without my even asking! What do you say we rent a movie and make some popcorn tonight?"

Later, as Denise prepared dinner, she noticed her oldest son quietly doing the job he'd forgotten to do earlier. And there was an umistakable warmth in the atmosphere that night. She smiled to herself. A little encouragement, she'd learned, made *everyone* feel good, and worked a lot better than nagging.

It's all too easy to take for granted the things that really matter, to focus on negatives, and to let others dictate our values. This world of ours often leads us to value superficial things. If you watch much television, you'll quickly learn that worthwhile people are beautiful, intelligent, athletic, wealthy, popular, talented—all sorts of things we and our children may not be. Learning to find and to appreciate the positive qualities in ourselves and our children will keep all of us centered and secure.

Begin to affirm yourself.

Affirmations—statements we repeat to ourselves until we make them a permanent part of our thinking—are a powerful sort of encouragement. To be effective, an affirmation needs to be something we can really believe or a statement we're willing to act as if we believe. Here are some affirmations that have helped parents heal their self-esteem:

"Expect a miracle."

"Work for progress, not perfection."

"I'm a worthwhile person in spite of my flaws and imperfections."

"One day at a time; one step at a time."

"This too will pass."

"It's okay to be a learner. I've got to crawl before I can walk."

"I'm not a bad parent. I'm just unskilled and skills can be acquired."

"I like the person I'm becoming."

Fred is a single dad; he's also a recovering alcoholic. When Fred was abusing alcohol, his children learned to be extremely demanding to get what they wanted — and it usually worked. When Fred went into recovery, he expected everything to miraculously change, but the kids didn't stop being demanding. Fred knew that giving in to them only made matters worse, but he didn't know what else to do. The nagging and whining began the moment he hit the front door after work, and Fred was almost at his wits' end. He was starting to think the effort wasn't worth it; perhaps a drink would solve his problems.

One day Fred picked up the phone and called his Alcoholics Anonymous sponsor. "I'm losing hope," he said sadly.

His sponsor chuckled and replied, "I remember feeling that way. But, Fred, it will pass. Not only that — you have to expect a miracle."

Fred snorted. "What do you mean, expect a miracle?"

His sponsor explained. "Some things are out of your control, but that doesn't mean they won't get better. Try telling yourself to expect a miracle every time you walk in the front door or when your kids start making their demands, and see what happens."

Fred was doubtful, but he didn't want to start drinking again. And he began to notice that the more he told himself to "expect a miracle," the less he noticed his kids' demands and the less he was affected by them. He started to see his children as miracles. He began to feel more loving towards them and began suggesting that they sit down and tell him about their day or that they all go out and play catch together before they started dinner. He and his children began to listen to each other, to talk more, and to complain less. Fred was surprised that such a simple step could have such powerful results.

As a single parent you may be giving yourself many negative, discouraging messages. Listen sometime to the conversations you have with yourself in front of the bathroom mirror or while you're driving. Do you focus on positive, hopeful things? Or are you reliving old battles, probing old wounds, and criticizing yourself for old mistakes? Sometimes it's easier simply to start a *new* habit of repeating affirmations than to change an old way of thinking. You probably know already what you need to hear and believe. Repeating these affirmations often during the day is a way to give yourself positive, encouraging messages.

Don't be afraid to change when it feels right to you.

Often there are habits in our lives — ways of thinking and behaving — that get us into trouble. Learning to look for the positive and to accept our own worth apart from our mistakes is important, but so is developing the courage to change.

Change of any sort is one of the most difficult and uncomfortable aspects of human life, and most of us resist it as long as we can. After all, a cozy rut or a bad habit may not be getting us anywhere, but at least it's familiar — we know what to expect even when we don't like it.

You'll know when it's time to make a change. Begin with small changes that you can make with success. For instance, if you want to be less critical, you can begin to comment on the positive traits of co-workers, family, and children. Success in meeting that goal will encourage you to tackle the next one — when you're ready.

Some changes feel so risky that we hesitate to make them even when we believe we should. Moving to a new city can be a frightening prospect for us and for our children: changing jobs, going back to school, finding a counselor, beginning a new relationship, or ending an old one are all big changes that require courage, and most people feel insecure at first. Having a support network, people you trust and can talk to, will help. So will success — making changes that work is the best encouragement of all!

Learn to value the moment.

It's all too easy, especially when we're in pain, to focus all of our energy on what happened yesterday, or on what we want to happen tomorrow. Unfortunately, however, our entire lives take place in the present. Each moment that we live is the *only* moment we have to enjoy; if our attention is always directed behind us or ahead of us, we'll never truly enjoy *now*, and we may miss much of what's happening in the world around us — and in our children's hearts and lives.

When you feel your thoughts running out of control into the future, or when you find yourself stuck in a past experience (again!), take a moment to breathe deeply several times and center yourself. When you can stay firmly rooted in the present, you'll be able to enjoy your lives and your children so much more, and you'll be more completely open to life's possibilities.

Take time to nurture yourself.

In most single-parent homes, there's one person who consistently seems to be overlooked and neglected: the parent! Single parents usually find themselves balancing work, domestic duties, child care, and goodness knows what else. Most report that they feel guilty about taking any time out for themselves, especially if it's just for fun.

But it's important to remember that we don't do our best work as parents when we're stressed out, tired, and frustrated. Each of us needs occasional "down time," moments when we can relax and get recharged. Besides, your children will learn to respect and value themselves (and you) if you show them that you respect and value yourself.

Begin by budgeting time each week for your own activities (see Chapter 3), and learn to treat yourself as a priority. You may discover that you approach parenting and work responsibilities with more energy and less resentment if you give yourself half an hour each evening to read a good book or soak in a hot bath—rather than cleaning the bathroom or ironing. Sure, a few household chores may have to wait, but they'll be done (eventually) by a more cheerful person.

Nurture your own creativity and uniqueness. Give yourself the freedom to do what you enjoy, whether it's gardening, tinkering with an old motorcycle, doing crafts or home decorating projects, or playing a musical instrument. Set up a babysitting co-op with neighborhood parents and take one evening each week to go out to a movie, sing in a choir, play softball, or take dancing lessons. Whatever it is that makes you feel energized and alive, make sure you find time to do it on a regular basis. It's not selfish; it's wisdom.

Just Do It!

Nadine had been on her own for three years. She was a devoted mother to her two sons, a conscientious employee, a regular churchgoer. Her apartment was usually clean, the bills were paid, and the kids never ran out of clean underwear. But, Nadine realized one day, she was bone-tired, and she wasn't having any fun.

Nadine mentioned her feelings to a good friend at work. "You used to love country-western dancing," her friend remarked. "Why don't you start doing that again?"

Nadine was shocked. "I couldn't go alone. Besides, what would I do with the boys?"

"I'll watch them. And you can watch my two another time when I want to go out." Nadine was clearly tempted, and her friend grinned at her. "Look, that new place downtown has free lessons on Tuesday nights. Tomorrow's Tuesday; bring the boys over after dinner and just *go!*"

And Nadine did. Her palms felt sweaty and her stomach was full of butterflies as she drove downtown the next night. Walking into the noisy dance hall was one of the hardest things she'd ever done. But once the music began, there wasn't time to be nervous. The room was full of people — some in couples, some alone — and Nadine found herself smiling as they learned the steps together. She discovered that she loved line dancing, which didn't even require a partner — and after a few Tuesdays had gone by, she found that her new friends included several prospective dance partners.

Nadine's co-workers (and her children) soon noticed that she had a new spring in her step and a much brighter smile. And Nadine discovered that the minor irritations of life didn't bother her the way they once had: after all, there was always Tuesday to look forward to!

Repairing and maintaining your self-esteem takes time and patience. But it will make you a much more contented parent, and a much healthier role model for your children.

Make Room for Growth

It may be hard to believe — in fact, you may not believe it's possible — but many single adults find that learning to live on their own opens doors and reveals possibilities that they hadn't anticipated. The day may come when a single mom sits down for an evening cup of tea after a busy, productive day and finds herself thinking unexpectedly, "I'm really happy." Or a single dad may stand gazing down at a sleeping child and find himself basking in a warm glow that he was too busy to notice before.

It's often change that breaks down the walls we've built for ourselves and helps us to become aware of all that is possible. Even if you didn't choose to become a single parent, you may one day find yourself with a new circle of friends, with abilities and talents you'd never acknowledged or explored before, perhaps with a new job or career goal. It can be fun to have a whole closet to oneself, never to find the toilet seat left up (or down!), to be able to choose brilliant turquoise paint or fuschia carpeting without asking anyone's permission.

Sometimes, though, children don't seem to be pleased by a single parent's newfound sense of peace and enjoyment. If Mom likes her new life too much, isn't that being disloyal to Dad? If Dad is too happy, does that mean he hates Mom? Are children being disloyal to one parent if they enjoy life with the other?

You can give yourself permission to enjoy the new positive parts of your life as you discover them — and there will be more and more as time passes. You can also give your children permission to take their own time adjusting by not making yourself overly responsible for their feelings, and you can help them to realize that each of us is responsible for his or her own happiness. Again, sensitivity to feelings (both your own and your children's) and a little patience will help you arrive at the day when life feels good to *all* of you.

Dealing with Loneliness

Reaching the point where life feels good can seem a long way off, and it's a rare single parent who has never struggled with feelings of isolation and loneliness. Evenings can be hard. What do you do when the children are finally asleep, the dishes and chores are done, and the house falls silent? It would be wonderful to have someone to talk to, but it's too late for the telephone. A movie would be fun, but how do you take the babysitter home without having to haul the children out of bed? Many single parents know how it feels to settle down for the evening with only the television for company and the depressing feeling that none of their friends (most of whom may be married) have any idea what being a single parent is really like.

All people feel alone occasionally, whether they're single or married. But loneliness seems to be a much more pressing problem when you're a single parent. And dealing with loneliness begins with examining your expectations. Sometimes, because society seems to be designed just for couples, we feel incomplete without a partner. No matter what we're doing or how much we might otherwise enjoy it, if we're doing it alone it just can't be fun.

Most of us learn eventually, however, that being with the wrong person can be worse than being alone. Many single parents forget how lonely they felt in their marriages. Often they didn't have time to feel the loneliness because they were so busy dealing with the problems. Amazingly enough, being alone can be a good thing. It can force us to develop our own strengths. It can — if we let it — give us opportunities to explore within ourselves, and to develop new ideas and abilities.

There are some positive steps you can take to combat the feeling of loneliness:

1. Build a network of friends, and make time to be with them. Simply having someone to talk to when you're feeling blue can make all the difference in the world.

2. When you're feeling cheerful, start a list of things you'd like to do, books you'd like to read, projects you'd like to begin. Then, when loneliness strikes, get out your list and get going. Having something constructive to focus your energy on can be a wonderful way to dissipate the blues.

3. Get involved with people — even if you don't feel like it. You can find many organizations and groups in your community that use volunteers, and many businesses encourage and allow time for employees to get involved. Spend an hour a week volunteering at a hospital or senior citizens' home. Tutor a student or mentor a young mother. Being involved in the lives of others will give you a new perspective on your own.

4. Take time to nurture yourself. Yes, it works here too!

5. Learn to be yourself, by yourself. It's tempting when you're single to believe that things would be better if only you had a partner to share your life. And it's

undeniably difficult when there's no one to hold you, touch you, or comfort you. But peace and contentment are things we all must find within ourselves, difficult as that may be. No one can *make* us happy. If you can find the strength to be truly comfortable alone, you'll be far better equipped to build a healthy relationship when someone special does wander into your life.

Making It on Your Own

All too often, Chris found being single an overwhelming experience. She'd been married for 18 years, and her divorce had been unexpected and painful. Both she and her children, Keith and Debbie, had gone through many difficult adjustments and Chris often felt terribly alone and hopelessly inadequate. She had purchased a small new house for herself and the children. Watching it being built filled her with hope, but moving in seemed to mean one job after another. Her ex-husband had been the handy one; Chris hardly knew one end of a hammer from the other, and had never been encouraged to learn. Still, settling into the new home gave Chris and the kids something to do together, something that was fresh and special and *theirs*.

One detail of the house was a constant annoyance. Chris had wanted a ceiling fan in the family room but couldn't afford to put one in right away. She'd requested that the builder wire it for her, and he had—but he'd left a bare light bulb right in the center of the ceiling to complete the circuit. The glare of that ugly bare bulb bothered Chris every time she turned it on.

Chris found a perfect ceiling fan on sale at the hardware store several months later. Her brother offered to come and install it for her, but he was often busy, and weeks went by while the fan sat in its box in a corner. At last a Saturday night arrived when Chris had had enough. The kids were with their dad, and Chris was feeling lonely and bored. Then her eye fell on the fan in its box.

"How hard can this be, anyway?" she thought as she ripped the box open.

It took hours, and Chris wanted to quit more than once. The instructions were in fractured English that she had trouble understanding, and the fan was large and hard to assemble alone. Her tools were inadequate. She had to make two calls to a neighbor to ask how to connect wires and where to find the circuit breaker. She almost fell off the ladder twice.

But when she flipped the switch and saw the fan's blades actually begin to turn, she felt a surge of elation and accomplishment she'd never experienced before. It worked! Even more miraculously, she'd done it *herself!* It was such fun to watch Keith's and Debbie's faces the next day when she showed them what she'd done.

It didn't seem all that important to anyone else, but for Chris it was a new beginning. She discovered not only that she could do things she hadn't thought possible, but that she really enjoyed working with her hands. She became a one-woman home improvement project. She painted jungle animals on the walls of the kids' bathroom. She acquired a drill and installed extra shelves in the bedroom closets. She planted roses and was thrilled when she cut the first blooms for her house; she joined a garden club to learn more, and met a wonderful new group of friends.

Best of all, Chris, Keith, and Debbie spent a weekend together building a front patio. They carried bags of sand, smoothed it, and placed paving stones on it. They put together inexpensive garden furniture and hung up a bird feeder and wind chimes. And they planted a rainbow of brightly colored flowers.

Chris and her children shared a pizza on the patio when it was finished, smiling happily at each other over the pepperoni. And suddenly Chris realized it was going to be okay. This life wasn't what she'd planned for herself and her children, and it wasn't exactly what she'd wanted — but it was going to be okay.

In fact, life was starting to feel *good* again. And that was the best accomplishment of all.

You may find that redefining your role as a single parent also redefines your role as a human being. Though change and growth can be painful at times, the finished product may be a person who couldn't have happened any other way, someone who is an inspiration and a joy to everyone. Keep your eyes and your mind open, try to enjoy the journey (bumps, wrong turns, and all), and watch what happens.

CHAPTER 10

Unmarried with Children: Social Life and Significant Others

Dave had had a wonderful night. He'd been out dancing with an old friend from college and he'd had more fun than he could remember in several years. As he whistled his way through the next morning, he realized that his daughter was not her usual cheerful self. Her lower lip protruded, her eyes wouldn't meet her father's, and Dave could have sworn he heard her muttering when his back was turned.

"Okay, Rachel," he finally said. "You've seemed unhappy all morning. Do you want to tell me what's bothering you?"

There was a long moment of silence; then, rather sullenly, she said, "I don't like you going out, Dad."

Dave sighed, exasperated. They'd been through this before. And Rachel had made several "get-acquainted" dinners positively miserable for Dave's helpless friends. He looked at his daughter's bowed head and felt a wave of both sympathy and frustration. He could understand her feelings, but he did his best to be a good father. Wasn't he entitled to have a life of his own sometimes?

As we've discussed, life for single parents can be a lonely thing. The months — and sometimes years — following a death or divorce are difficult ones. Living (and parenting) alone can be like building a fortress: the longer we stay in it, the harder it can be to come out. It can be hard to meet people, scary to trust them, tricky to overcome lingering feelings of hurt, rejection, or guilt.

And that's not all — the logistical problems can be overwhelming. How do you squeeze time for dinner and a movie into a week that already contains work, housework, and (hopefully) time with your children? What about money? And child care?

Single parents need lives of their own, though, and eventually most do find themselves ready to tackle the dating game. Like Dave, many single parents also find that their children aren't exactly thrilled with the concept. And when children are feeling insecure, they often show it by inventing new and wonderful forms of misbehavior.

But Why Do My Kids Act That Way?

It's really not hard to understand why so many children find their parents' social lives threatening. A child's entire world is built around his relationship with his parents, and their relationship with each other. When those parents are no longer together, for whatever reason — when life, security, and belonging depend on *one* parent — the world can become a fragile and unstable place. We may tell our children, "I love you and I would never leave you." But to a child who has already experienced the loss of one parent, those words may provide little comfort.

It's normal for a child to cling to her parent, to feel a sense of ownership, and to be jealous of people and things that deflect that parent's attention. Many single parents have had the experience of introducing their sons and daughters to a new friend and being met with either indifference or outright hostility. Then again, some children go to the opposite extreme, trying relentlessly to find a new "mommy" or "daddy," someone to fill the void in their own and their parent's lives. Either reaction can make parents and their friends terribly uncomfortable.

Does that mean you give up the entire idea? Or that you go out only when your children aren't around? It's easy for single parents to choose one extreme or the other—being totally insensitive to the feelings of their children, or overreacting to the demands of their children and allowing themselves to be manipulated to unhealthy extremes. How can single parents ease the transition into new relationships, both for themselves and for their children?

Monica had just met an interesting, exciting new man. Her enthusiasm and happiness were obvious when she told 13-year-old Jesse and 9-year-old Samantha that she was planning to go with her new friend to an out-of-town concert. She was startled and a little angry when Jesse announced, in an authoritative tone, "You can't go out of town with this guy."

Monica knew this was not the time to take Jesse on, so she said only, "We'll talk about this later." That evening she went into Jesse's room, where he was doing his homework, turned down the stereo a little, and said, "Are you ready to have a little talk with me now?"

Jesse looked up at his mother, then returned his gaze to his book. "I guess so," was all he said.

Monica took a deep breath and began. "Honey, first I need to tell you that I'm the mom, and it's not okay for you to tell me what I can or can't do. But second, I really value your opinion and want to hear your thoughts and feelings. Do you want to tell me why you don't want me to go to this concert with my new friend?"

Jesse looked directly into his mother's eyes. "You don't know this man very well, Mom. How do you know you can trust him?"

Her son's evident concern and love touched Monica's heart. "Honey, that's a very good point. I *don't* know him very well. I have a good feeling about him, but I don't know him yet. Would it make you feel better if we went with another couple whom I do know? Come to think of it, that would make *me* feel better!"

Jesse grinned. "I think that would be very smart, Mom."

Monica added, "And how would you like it if I invited him over for dinner first, so we can all get to know him a little better? After all, I know I can trust your opinion."

Jesse sat up a little straighter. "If you want to," he said.

Monica used this conflict with her son as an opportunity to build closeness. First she waited through a "cooling-off" period instead of trying to deal with the problem when emotions were high. Then she kindly and firmly established the boundaries between parent and child. Next, she let Jesse know that she valued his opinion and demonstrated the truth of that statement by incorporating his opinion into a plan. Finally, through this interaction, she taught Jesse how to express his opinions in ways that are respectful and helpful. What could have been a major conflict turned out to be an opportunity to enrich her relationship with her son. Unsolicited advice, however, is not always so helpful.

Dating with an Audience

Most single parents get a great deal of advice — both solicited and unsolicited — on the subject of dating. Everyone, from family to friends to ex-spouses, has an opinion: "The sooner you get remarried, the better — your kids need a whole family." "Don't rush into anything — you don't want to make another mistake!" "Always bring your dates home. You need to find out from the beginning whether they're good with your kids." "Don't let your children meet your dates unless the relationship is serious. Too many people coming in and out of their lives is upsetting and they'll be hurt if you break up with someone they've become attached to." "Keep your private life away from your children — you don't want to give them ideas." "Enjoy your sexuality while you can. And it will teach your kids not to have hang-ups."

Where on earth does the truth lie? Adult relationships are rarely simple, and they seem to be even less so when children are involved. Dating too soon, while a child is grieving over the loss of one parent, can cause unnecessary pain. Not dating at all can cause both parent and child to doubt that relationships are healthy or necessary. In the end, each parent must decide what's comfortable, what feels right, and what balances the needs and feelings of both adults and children. The answer will probably be different in each family, but there are several things to keep in mind.

Work Toward Understanding

Change can be difficult for both adults and children, and frequently children in single-parent homes have experienced many changes in their short lives. Perhaps the most helpful thing you can do is to make an effort to understand how your children are *feeling* about your other relationships. If you can see that your children may be afraid of losing you, that they worry about you, that they feel threatened or replaced or jealous, then you can deal honestly with their feelings, letting them know you understand and using emotional honesty to help them understand you.

Remember Dave? He discussed his frustration over Rachel's resistance to his social life with a group of single friends at lunch one day. They were able to give him a number of helpful suggestions, ideas all single parents might want to keep in mind:

1. Take time to listen to your child without defensiveness or explanations and use reflective listening so that she feels understood (see Chapter 2). Whether or not you agree with them, your child's perceptions have a lot to do with how she acts. Once a child knows her parent

understands and accepts her feelings, she may have less need to demonstrate them through troubling behavior.

2. Ask your child if she would now be willing to listen to you. Children are usually more open when they've agreed to listen and when they feel listened to themselves. Your child may need to see that having friends is just as important to you as it is to her. You may choose to explain what a particular relationship means to you and what is — or is not — happening. Be honest — it will save untold trouble later on. But be aware too that it's important not to talk *too* much; the young people in your home don't need to know the intimate details of your relationships.

   Remember that you're always your child's number one role model. "Do as I say, not as I do" doesn't hold much water these days, especially with teenagers. Be sure you conduct your relationships in a way you wouldn't mind your children conducting theirs.

3. Don't engage in conduct you're ashamed of. Some single parents develop an unhealthy pattern of secrecy (with the rationalization that their children don't need to know all the details) when the truth is that they're doing something they aren't proud of.

   If you're uneasy with any aspect of an adult relationship, it may be better to take your time. For example, some parents are comfortable having a friend spend the night while their children are with them; others choose not to sleep with a friend, or to do so only when the children are with the other parent. Whatever you decide to do, be sure you feel comfortable with your actions. If you find you must lie or bend the truth to explain a relationship to your children or friends, that relationship may not be a healthy one for you — or at least not yet.

4. Make sure your actions match your words. When you tell your children "You're important to me," but somehow never make room in your life for special time with them, children don't feel important at all and may react with resentment and hostility. If you have a "significant other" who's included in everything, a child can feel pushed out. Be sure you spend time with your child alone, whether it's doing special things, talking, or just hanging out.

5. Do some problem solving to find solutions that work for everyone concerned. Plan ways for you and your children to have time together, time alone, and time with friends. If you're seeing someone who is a regular part of your life, include him or her in a family meeting with your children and have everyone share in the compliments, the brainstorming, and the plans for special activities (see Chapter 8).

6. Above all, be patient. It takes time to adjust to change, to new relationships, and to new ideas. Most children eventually figure out that a parent who is happy and interested in life is a whole lot easier to get along with than one who's depressed and isolated.

Single Parents and Sexuality

There it is: the "S" word. In a world where teens (and even pre-teens) experiment with sex, where sex is used to sell everything from beer to cosmetics to coffee, and where the consequences of unsafe sex can be so devastating, it's not surprising that single parents are often unsure of how to feel, what to think, and how to proceed with a relationship. Is there a "right" way or a "wrong" way? Although advice on intimate relationships is outside the scope of this book, there are a couple of ideas that may help you make healthy decisions about life as a single adult

— particularly as a single parent with a young audience watching your every move.

Kathleen was 38 when her husband died of cancer. The final stages of his illness had been traumatic for the entire family. Their grief was strong, and sometimes it felt as though the grieving would never end. For the first year it was easy for Kathleen to lose herself in her children and her work—staying busy eased the pain.

"For a long, long time," she told a friend over lunch one day, "I never even thought about sex. Oh, sometimes I missed being held and loved. Doug and I had such a good relationship. But I just felt so sad and empty that the idea of having sex never crossed my mind. I'm not unattractive, and I suppose I could have gone out occasionally. I guess I was just numb.

"But all of a sudden," Kathleen continued with some embarrassment, "it seems to be all I think about. If I go to a movie or read a novel, the sexy parts really affect me. I'm starting to think I'm obsessed. What am I supposed to do? Is there something wrong with me?"

Many single parents, male and female, can identify with Kathleen. The death of a spouse or the emotional upheaval associated with a divorce can kill sexual feelings for months or even years, even in a person who has enjoyed an active sex life during marriage. Other things seem much more important: making sure the children are adjusting, dealing with job stress, all of those pressures we're so familiar with. Sooner or later, however, frozen feelings begin to thaw. Having a physical relationship with someone not only begins to seem possible—it may begin to seem necessary!

Remember that sexuality is a normal part of adult life and sexual feelings are perfectly healthy. You're the only person who can decide whether or not you want your relationships to include sex and how you'll handle that, but it's normal to feel the desire for human contact.

Remember that your children will form their own decisions about what's right and wrong by watching you. What they observe in your relationship with a new partner may be very different from what they observed in the last stages of your marriage, and it may be wise to check their perceptions and feelings occasionally. Even when they like your new "friend," children may believe that kissing, holding hands, or other forms of touching are "disloyal" to the missing parent. Open communication, reflective listening, sensitivity, and a little patience will help you work through these issues together.

Remember, too, that you're highly vulnerable in the aftermath of a death or divorce, or when you've been alone for a long period of time. All too often, single adults suffer from a low sense of self-worth and become involved in a relationship they're not ready for (or that they're ashamed of later) because having someone want their company is so intoxicating. It's easy to become involved romantically (and sexually) with a sympathetic friend, an attorney, a counselor, or a casual acquaintance when you've been alone or when you've been hurt. It's undoubtedly easier said than done, but try to be very gentle with yourself, and don't be afraid to move slowly.

As much as possible, try not to think of everyone you meet as a potential mate. Most single adults feel a bit desperate at times, particularly if they've been alone for a while or if close friends (or an ex-spouse) seem to be marrying or finding romance. Sometimes we evaluate co-workers, fellow students, neighbors, or people we meet at church solely on the basis of their attractiveness or their suitability as a partner. Making judgments in that way can cause us to disregard people who might prove to be wonderful friends, part of the support network that all single parents need. If you're taking time to nurture yourself and getting involved in things you enjoy, the chances are good that you'll meet people who will prove to be wonderful friends or, possibly, more than friends.

"But," you may be wondering, "what if I do meet someone I want to become involved with? Is there a right way—or a wrong way—to handle that relationship with my children? If I become sexually active, will they assume that's okay for them too? I'd like to have an adult relationship, but I'm not sure I'm comfortable with my *kids* having one!"

Sorting out relationships and the ways children will react to them can be difficult. Randy had been separated from his wife, Mary, for only one month when he met Leigh. Sparks flew when Leigh and Randy were together — they felt an immediate passion for each other and soon were spending all of their free time together. Randy was eager to introduce Leigh to his seven-year-old daughter, Sarah, who was coming for her weekend visit with her dad. He knew Sarah was still struggling with her parents' decision to separate, but he felt sure she'd love Leigh, and he thought the coming weekend would be a great time for them to get acquainted.

The weekend, however, didn't go smoothly. Randy was so in love that he couldn't seem to keep his hands off his girlfriend. As Sarah watched, she felt more and more embarrassed; her dad certainly had never acted this way with her mom. Randy invited Leigh to spend the night without a second thought, and Sarah grew more uncomfortable by the minute. When her dad tucked her into bed, he said with a grin, "Isn't Leigh great, honey?" Sarah nodded silently, blinking back confused, angry tears.

When Sarah woke up the next morning, she forgot all about Leigh — until she skipped into her dad's bedroom to say good morning and found him making love to Leigh. Sarah's words died in her throat. Confused and frightened, she ran back to her room crying. She called her mother and pleaded with her to come pick her up early.

Sarah came home from her dad's house feeling both neglected and sickened by Randy's behavior with Leigh. Mary, Sarah's mother, was angry, and immediately called her attorney to ask that Sarah's visits with her father be restricted.

A judge later determined that Sarah needed time to adjust to her parents' divorce, that it was in her best interests that her visits with her father occur only if he had no guests — and that she shouldn't visit overnight for six months.

Randy's enthusiasm for his new love was understandable, but he forgot to consider Sarah's feelings. This does not mean that children should rule the household and that parents should never do anything their children don't like. However, if Randy had considered Sarah's vulnerability, he might have moved with more caution, allowing Sarah time to adjust at her own pace. Sarah might never have liked Leigh, even if her father had been less demonstrative; it's hard for most children to watch someone take the place of their mother or father. However, children can learn to accept other adults in their lives, in time, when parents are considerate and respectful of both their own needs *and* the needs of their children.

But Can You Keep Everyone Happy?

Even when a relationship is healthy, working out the details can be difficult for everyone concerned. Janet collapsed into a chair at her single parents' group one evening with a sigh. The group facilitator laughed. "Looks like you might have a problem, Janet," she said.

Janet sighed again. "I don't know whether having a boy-friend is worth the trouble." She laughed, "What a dumb term for a 45-year-old man, but 'significant other'? Anyway, my daughter Jessica loves Steve. When he comes to visit, Jessica is all over us, wanting our attention and interrupting everything we try to do. I told her I wanted to spend time alone with Steve, but she says he's her boyfriend and she wants time alone with him too. In fact, she wants him to be her daddy.

"What should I do? Steve and I are in an exclusive relationship, but I'm afraid to let Jessica get too attached to him because I don't know if we'll get married. I don't want her to be hurt if we end the relationship. And occasionally I'd like some time alone with Steve. Do we always have to go out to be alone?"

A number of heads nodded vigorously as Janet finished; others had had the same problem.

"Why don't we see if we can come up with some solutions to Janet's problem?" the facilitator asked. It wasn't hard for the group, with their variety of experiences, to offer some suggestions. Janet heard several ideas she wanted to try. When Janet arrived at the next week's meeting she told them what had happened.

"Steve and I decided to have a family meeting with Jessica (even though I felt a little awkward including an 'outsider' in a family meeting). I took some time to tell Jessica how much I'd appreciated her help around the house that week. Then each of us got a chance to say what we felt and what we wanted from our relationships. It was interesting—I learned some things about both Steve and Jessica that I might never have known otherwise. Then we decided to brainstorm some ideas about how we could spend our time so that no one felt left out.

"We planned some things that Jessica and I would do alone together—she wanted to go for ice cream after school and maybe to the park—and we talked about some things that Steve and I had planned to do on our own. Then we agreed that when Steve comes over to our house, he and Jessica will spend ten minutes alone together, maybe to read a story or play a game.

"We agreed that after Jessica's time with Steve we'll all have dinner together. Then Jessica will leave, to let us have some time alone. She said it would help her if she could have a friend over —I'd never thought of that. We also agreed that Jessica would be allowed to interrupt us three times. After all, she needs to know that I'm not too busy for her. Our agreements seem to be working pretty well so far, and it feels more comfortable for all of us now when Steve comes over. And if it stops working, we'll just discuss it again at the next family meeting."

Janet's experience incorporates several principles of effective parenting:

1. Children need to know that they matter to you, and that they still have access to you even when you're busy or with someone else. If the access isn't planned, they'll take it

anyway with constant demands for attention. Also, when kids help plan the number of interruptions they can have, they seldom use their total allotment. Involvement invites cooperation.

2. Children feel belonging and significance when they're included in problem-solving or planning sessions. And when they feel they belong, they're less likely to feel discouraged — and less likely to misbehave.

3. When a difficult situation arises, decide what *you* will do instead of what you'll make your children do. Trying to make children do something often invites power struggles. Letting children know your expectations in advance gives them the opportunity to choose their responses — and to experience the consequences of their choices. It's important to follow through with kindness and firmness. Firmness requires action; kindness requires eliminating lectures and put-downs.

Jessica was willing to cooperate because she felt a sense of belonging and involvement — and because she felt loved. Making sure the message of love gets through is so very important, yet in the midst of our busy lives and new relationships it's often harder to do than we think.

Dealing with the Belief Behind the Behavior

Behavior never happens in a vacuum — there are always beliefs and feelings behind it. Anne, a single mother with a new love in her life, found a special way of getting past her son's behavior to the belief behind it.

Anne was nervous about bringing Richard home to meet her sons, but he was a wonderful man and she was fairly sure her boys would like him. Jeff, her older son, accepted Richard with enthusiasm but Jonathan, her little one, reacted with outright hostility.

"We don't need you here," he said to the startled Richard. Then he disappeared into his room with a resounding thud of the door.

Anne was surprised and embarrassed, but she realized that Jonathan was probably afraid—afraid of changing their life together, afraid that if Mom loved someone new she'd love him less, afraid that nothing would be right anymore.

One evening, after dinner had been eaten and all the evening's work was finished, Anne sat down with Jonathan. "Would you like to hear a story?" she asked. "This one is about our family."

As the little boy snuggled against her side, Anne smiled at Jeff, who was sitting across the room, and lit a tall candle.

"These candles represent our family," she told the boys. "This tall one is for me." She lit the candle with a match. "This flame represents my love."

"It's bright," Jonathan said, entranced by the flickering flame.

"It is," his mother agreed. "That's because I have so much love in me." Anne picked up a smaller candle and lit it with the flame from her own. "This candle is your big brother Jeff. When he was born, I gave him all my love. But look—I still had all my love left."

She put the candle in a holder and picked up a smaller one. "This candle is you, Jonathan."

"It's red," the little boy said delightedly. "That's my favorite color!"

Anne smiled and ruffled his hair, and lit his little red candle from her tall one. "When you were born, I gave you all my love. Jeff still has all my love, and I still have all my love left. See all the bright love we have in this family?"

Then Anne picked up another tall candle and used the flame from her own to light it. "Now I'm giving my love to Richard. You still have all my love, Jeff still has all my love, and

I still have all my love left. That's the way love works. The more you give away, the more you have. Every candle added to the family just brings more love into our home. Richard is someone new and it will take you some time to get to know him. But I have plenty of love for all of you."

Anne and the boys were quiet for a moment, watching the flames and letting the message sink in. Then Jonathan gave his mom a big hug and went off to get ready for bed.

There would still be problems to be solved and adjustments to be made. There would undoubtedly be rough spots ahead. But understanding that his mother had plenty of love to share made Jonathan feel far less vulnerable, and increased the chances that he could eventually accept a new person in his family.

Facing the changes that occur in a family can be a complicated process, but it can also be an opportunity to build a truly special and lasting relationship with your children and to teach them understanding and coping skills they'll have for a lifetime. If it takes more time than you'd like, try to be patient. Your children may believe you're their only lifeline and they may be reluctant to release you to a life — and relationships — of your own. But you'll all be healthier in the long run if your life balances the well-being of your children with your own happiness and contentment. Learn to listen with your heart as well as your head, and eventually that balance will come.

CHAPTER 11

Your Child's Other Parent: In or Out of the Picture?

For the vast majority of single parents, single parenthood is the result of a divorce. That means that out there somewhere is the children's other parent. And that, in turn, means all sorts of complicated problems and feelings.

How do we get along now that we're not married? How do we handle visitation, custody, new relationships in either household? What do we do if we simply can't stand each other? What if my child's other parent never visits, never calls, doesn't care? What if he or she never contributes to our children's support? And what do I tell my children?

Coping with Divorce

Divorce is a highly traumatic event in *anyone's* life. It can mean not only the separation of a couple and their children, but new homes, new jobs, new living conditions, new lives, lower income. Most divorcing parents are told that children have the best chance of emerging from divorce whole and healthy when the parents can build an amicable relationship, when the children can love and be with both parents, and when they're spared open hostility between two people they love. However, most divorcing parents are so caught up in their personal pain and/or anger that they rarely think about their children. Newly divorced parents are frequently trying to meet their children's needs at a time when major decisions must be made and when their own emotional resources are at a low ebb. It can be exhausting.

"Build an amicable relationship" sounds good. But whatever the reasons you divorced, the inevitably tangled emotions can make it all but impossible. "You don't know my ex-wife," mutters one man. "I'm willing to try," a woman chimes in, "but my ex-husband does everything he can to hurt me."

Most parents love their children and worry about the effects a divorce will have on them. Most are aware that open hostility, negative and critical remarks about the absent parent (even when they're true), and manipulative actions and comments can be devastating to children. Yet sometimes the temptation to strike back can be irresistible. Many times parents fear that the only way to keep their children's love is to compete — to show more love, buy more gifts, do more for the child than the other parent. Children, bewildered, hurting, and often blaming themselves, can become the most potent weapons between warring parents — and the ultimate victims.

When you share a child with someone, that person is a part of your life for years, like it or not. Overcoming hurt, anger, disappointment, jealousy, guilt, and regret enough to carry on a civil relationship with that person can seem impossible. Yes, too many parents disappear, don't care, don't pay support. But some parents do wish they could be involved in their children's lives and wish they could find a new way to relate to their ex-spouse.

Is it really possible? Can divorced parents share their children's lives? Can they show up at school programs, high school graduations, or weddings without having to sit at opposite ends of the room? Can they discuss problems at school, illness, or financial arrangements without fighting the same old battles? Is it possible for wounded adults to put their children first?

Not always, perhaps; after all, we're human, we have our own needs, and we do make mistakes. But building a working relationship after divorce *is* possible, and both children and adults are invariably better off for it.

Building a Working Partnership

Divorce is not the end of parenting. It marks a change in direction, but the opportunity remains to raise children who know they have two parents who love them. Healing, forgiveness, and rebuilding an old relationship in a new form take time and a great deal of commitment, when these things are possible at all—and, unfortunately, not all stories have happy endings. Facing hurts and old memories is painful, and that pain doesn't fade as quickly as we might wish. Still, our children's emotional health and well-being remains the best reason to work at making things different. But how?

It simply isn't true that parents who couldn't get along as marriage partners can't work together as parents. They can. But working together as parents means breaking the old patterns of relating to one another and learning new ones. It means cooperating with the other parent in raising the children, no matter how they feel about each other. It means sharing an interest in children's activities and feelings, sharing responsibility for their care, respecting each other's rights and privacy, and developing ways to communicate about the children's needs and problems. It also means accepting the difficult truth that you probably can't change either your ex-spouse or the way he or she chooses to run a household.

A Word About Fathers

There are many dedicated single fathers, both custodial and noncustodial, who devote endless time, energy, and resources to their children. These fathers share both the frustrations and the joys of watching their children grow and develop, and they deserve to be acknowledged and encouraged. Statistics, however, tell us some interesting things. More than a quarter of all children under the age of 18 live in single-parent homes — and the overwhelming majority of those single parents are mothers. Sadly, statistics also tell us that almost half of all divorced fathers fail to see their children regularly, and two-thirds fail to support them adequately. The results for children, economically and emotionally, are devastating.

American culture over the years has tended to minimize the importance of fathers. We have traditionally viewed raising children, especially young ones, as women's work. Though that perception is changing, it remains true that changing diapers, spooning strained vegetables, and walking the floor with a crying infant are not exactly perceived as masculine endeavors.

Fathers often become more involved as their children grow older, but what matters most is consistency and regular participation in the rhythms and rituals of everyday life. Fathers play crucial roles in the emotional, moral, and intellectual development of their children, and their absence creates a void.

Do children need their mothers? Absolutely. Can stepfathers and close family friends help fill the gap and provide positive male role models? Certainly. Yet the bottom line remains unchanged: no one can truly replace a child's father. And even when a child, a teenager, a young adult, has not seen his or her father for years, the yearning may remain. Sometimes a sense of betrayal and abandonment remains as well, and that can cripple a child's willingness to trust, or to risk marriage and parenthood himself.

The legal issues of support and visitation are beyond the scope of this book; however, a few general facts may be helpful. Though laws differ from state to state, some concepts are standard. Although the law generally states that parents cannot be compelled to visit children, they do have a legal obligation to provide support. If you're not receiving the child support you're entitled to, you should make every effort to have the support provisions of your divorce decree enforced; it's in both your own and your children's best interests. The best place to enforce child support provisions is at the District Attorney's office for the county where the support order was filed.

The law also acknowledges that children do best when they have continuous and frequent contact with both parents. Only if evidence exists proving that visitation would actually harm a child will the courts restrict a parent's right to visitation. If you have serious disputes with your children's other parent about these issues, a possible solution lies in mediation by an objective third party. Your local family law court can give you information about mediation in your area.

If you're a father, you have a critical part to play in your children's lives — and no one can play that particular part but you. If you've been absent from your children's lives, it's never too late to begin. There may never again be as good a time as *now*.

The Noncustodial Parent

In an ideal world, children enjoy the active love and involvement of *both* parents. If you're a noncustodial parent, it may be difficult for you to participate regularly in your children's lives. If you live at a distance, your contact with your children may be limited to summer and holiday visits. Still, there are ways to remain a vital part of their lives. Regular phone calls are a wonderful way to stay in touch. Letters and cards can be kept, reread, and treasured. Even the fax machine can come in handy!

One father gave his children a fax machine for Christmas and regularly sends notes, drawings, cartoons, and messages from wherever he happens to be.

If you travel without your children or live far away from them, sending a "treasure box" filled with shells, leaves, rocks, or small souvenirs from the places you visit can let them know that they're always in your thoughts and close to your heart. Try sending a double-entry journal back and forth, recording your activities and thoughts and leaving room for your children to record theirs. Anything that keeps you tuned in and in touch is well worth the effort it takes.

It's sometimes difficult to *feel* like a parent when you don't have custody of your children. Sometimes their feelings and behavior can be harder to deal with when your time together is limited, and you may begin to feel that an occasional weekend is hardly worth the effort. But if you don't have a lot of time together, work at improving the *quality* of the time you spend. Do simple things, but do them together. Share *yourself* with your children: teach them your skills, involve them in your hobbies and interests, show them who you are and what you do, and let them be a part of your life. The best solution is probably the hardest to find: a balance of continuity and consistency, love and attention.

Try to end each visitation on a positive note. Children often fear that their noncustodial parent won't want to see them again if they misbehave, and parents sometimes use that threat to motivate children to behave properly. Your children are less likely to feel rejected if you resolve any differences *before* they leave. Making family meetings a part of the time you spend together can help.

If it's at all possible, try to work with your child's other parent at raising your children. Show that you're interested in child-care decisions, school events, religious training. Offer your opinions without criticizing those of your former mate. You might try giving the other parent a copy of this book, attending the same parenting class (perhaps at different times!), or finding other ways to create a consistent environment for the children you love.

Try to remember, even when the going is tough, that your children have only two parents, and that you're one of them — an irreplaceable part of who they are. Continuing to be involved after a divorce can be difficult, even painful, for both mothers and fathers, yet it may be the greatest gift you ever give your children.

Avoiding the Pitfalls of Post-Divorce Parenting

No one can tell you exactly how to build a working partnership with your children's other parent; it takes trial and error, effort and commitment. There are, however, a few pitfalls to mark and avoid. Each is discussed here:

1. Respect your child's need to love and spend time with the other parent.

2. Resist the temptation to use your children as spies.

3. Recognize and accept that you cannot control your child's other parent.

Respect your child's need to love and spend time with the other parent.

Children are amazing people; they have the ability to see their parents' faults and flaws clearly and yet to love them anyway. They may know, for instance, that Dad often breaks his promises, or that Mom is flaky and unreliable. Still, they also know that their parents are part of who *they* are; criticizing or ridiculing a child's other parent is the same as criticizing *a part of the child*. And most children will continue to love their parents despite neglect, broken promises, and human failure.

Parents are often insecure and vulnerable in the aftermath of a divorce, and it can be tempting to influence a child's loyalty by demeaning the other parent, or by being possessive and controlling. It helps to remember that wanting to see and spend time with the other parent doesn't mean your child is betraying you, or that she doesn't love *you*. Our feelings are so easily hurt when circumstances require us to give up time with our children, even for a weekend. Unfortunately, children often wind up afraid to love Mom when they're with Dad, afraid to love Dad when they're with Mom, and afraid to let either parent know that they enjoy being with the other. Life becomes a balancing act, trying to keep both parents happy and secure — and the ultimate loser will be the child.

Sometimes, too, a noncustodial parent who wants to be involved in a child's life is shut out by an insecure custodial parent. Not only does the child lose the opportunity for a life with two active parents, but the custodial parent may lose a valuable source of support, help, and advice.

Occasionally the noncustodial parent fights for the children's loyalty by being the "good" parent, providing special treats and outings every time they're together. This makes life difficult both for the children, who need order and daily routines, and for the custodial parent, who may resent being the one responsible for day-to-day discipline and maintenance. (It eventually becomes difficult for the "good" parent also, since children will learn to expect special treats all the time.)

The experience of divorce is entirely different for children than it is for parents. Children base their entire world on their family structure. When that structure collapses, the children's world is temporarily without supports. Children have a compressed sense of time — they don't understand that the chaos is temporary. What they do know is that they're dependent on the family and that the family has now fallen apart. They're left with a feeling of helplessness. They can't prevent the divorce, fix it, or rescue Mom or Dad. No one gives priority to their wishes, concerns, and fears. Children often feel intense loneliness. Divorce is an acutely painful, long-remembered experience that children often endure with the uncomfortable feeling that they're alone in the world.

Try not to seek revenge for your own hurts through your children. Try to remember that saying degrading things about the other parent to your children is far more destructive to them than it is to that other parent. Encourage your children to love and respect both of you. Let them know they're not being disloyal to you by loving their other parent also.

Remember, too, that it's normal for children to want their parents to be together — and that they may make some efforts to engineer a reconciliation. Frustrating and embarrassing as these efforts may be for you, you can recognize your children's feelings with compassion and understanding while still being honest about your situation (see Chapter 2).

Resist the temptation to use your children as spies.

It's difficult not to be curious about what goes on in the other parent's home. For instance, when your ex-spouse begins a new relationship, you may find yourself struggling with hurt, bitterness, anger, or rejection. The idea that *that person* is out there finding love and romance with someone new can be like a pebble in your shoe — a constant irritation.

The temptation arises when we realize our children know exactly what's going on at our ex-spouse's house and all we need to do is ask one little question . . .

Eddie came home from his mom's house one morning and announced that he and Mom had had a wonderful evening with Jerry, Mom's new boyfriend.

"We went out for pizza," Eddie said, "and then we played a game together." Then he added innocently, "And then Jerry spent the night with us." And Dad, hurting, jealous, and a little bit angry, said, "Oh yeah? And where did he sleep?"

It doesn't matter how Eddie answers. As we've mentioned, children have incredibly sensitive antennas where their parents' feelings and motives are concerned, and by the time Dad's question had registered, Eddie was already weighing the consequences of his answer—and squirming inside. The only way he could avoid betraying his mother while satisfying his father's curiosity was to lie, or to say "I don't know."

Children caught between two parents live with a sense of conflicting loyalties, loving both, wanting to protect the one who's hurting, wanting to avoid conflict. Even if the relationship between ex-spouses is friendly, there are inevitable differences in life in the two households and the knowledge that our children could be sources of "inside information" can be overwhelming.

But employing our children as spies is a dangerous business. Most children want to be free to love both parents and to participate fully in both homes—to have two "families." Being used by Mom as a weapon against Dad, or by Dad as a spy in Mom's house, is painful and uncomfortable, and children often resort to keeping the two halves of their family as separate as possible, not talking to one parent about what the other is doing for fear of causing hurt or anger. And "don't talk" rules, wherever they come from, can be emotionally devastating.

What's a single parent to do? Perhaps the best thing is to develop his own antenna, to become aware and "tuned in" to his child's feelings, and then to be willing to work with those feelings. When we can understand the whole situation and the feelings of everyone involved, we can at least talk—and reach the understanding that leaves room for healing to take place.

Beth was driving her young son, Mark, home from school one afternoon. Mark's father had just told her he planned to take Mark with him to visit his new girlfriend and her children in Arizona for Christmas. Christmas was only a month away, but Mark had yet to mention the trip to his mom, and Beth's instincts told her that she needed to help him talk about it. Although Beth wasn't at all sure *she* was happy about the prospect of spending Christmas alone while her only son was with his father, she knew she had to make it okay for Mark to go happily, and to enjoy his time with his dad.

"You'll probably have a wonderful time with Dad and Carol at Christmas," Beth said conversationally as they pulled away from the school. Mark turned to her with shock written all over his face. "You know about that?" he asked. And as Beth watched, his shoulders sagged in obvious relief.

Beth's antenna gave her the clues she needed to make sense of Mark's reaction. "Were you afraid to tell me about your trip because you were afraid it would hurt my feelings?" she asked. Mark nodded, still shy about saying too much.

Beth was then able to explain how she did feel. "How would you feel if your best friend suddenly had a new friend and didn't want to play with you ever again?" Mark knew the answer right away. "I'd feel bad," he said simply.

"Well," Beth continued quietly, "I still feel a little hurt that your Dad doesn't want to be with me anymore. But I understand that you love him, and that you really like Carol, and that you're looking forward to your trip. I *want* you to be happy, honey."

It took time, but Mark began to realize that his mom could accept his feelings even though her own were different. Gradually he began to talk freely about his other home and his new "family." It wasn't always easy for Beth to hear, but she was genuinely glad that Mark felt comfortable being honest with her and that he no longer felt he had to hide part of his life from her. As long as she could see that he was content and thriving, she knew there was little in the other home she needed to be concerned about—and no need to use Mark as a spy.

Careful attention—without prying—to the verbal and nonverbal clues your children give you will also tell you when you *do* need to know what's going on in the other parent's house, and you can deal with that situation if it arises. Building an honest relationship of love and closeness and keeping the lines of communication open are the best ways to make sure your children are doing well.

Recognize and accept that you cannot control your child's other parent.

Susan's two daughters were up and dressed early Saturday morning. Today their dad was coming to spend the day with them. They barely watched the Saturday-morning cartoons — their ears were tuned for the sound of the doorbell and they got up frequently to look down the street. Susan watched helplessly as the clock ticked on, the cartoons ended, and lunchtime came and went. She watched her daughters' smiles and excitement fade, watched their heads droop. She didn't know what to say to them, so she bustled busily around the house, stopping occasionally to pat their heads or hug them while having angry mental conversations with their father.

It was mid-afternoon when Robert, the girls' dad, finally arrived, looking more than a little guilty. Susan, her daughters' disappointment fresh in her mind, lit into him the moment the door opened.

"Where *were* you?" she shouted. "Didn't you know the girls were waiting for you? Why didn't you call? You've *always* been like this! If you can't keep your promises to your kids, maybe you shouldn't have *any* visitation."

"I'd promised to take my girlfriend and her kids to lunch. I forgot all about it. Quit nagging me!" Robert felt defensive and ashamed and hid it beneath a cloak of anger, shouting just as loudly as Susan. And as their parents argued over their heads, the two girls stood looking at their shoes and fidgeting with their clothing, silently wishing they could be somewhere else, far away from the shouting and the disappointment.

Married couples raising children disagree occasionally, or have differing opinions on parenting. But somehow, when couples divorce, those differences seem to be magnified. It's hard not to want to control what happens in the other parent's house, or to force the other parent to change somehow. And it's difficult to accept the fact that such changes are almost impossible to make.

"But my ex-wife is so permissive—she spoils those kids rotten," one dad may say. "My kids' dad is too strict. I hate to send them there because he's so hard on them," a mom responds. "My ex-husband never sees the kids." "My children's mom only cares about her boyfriend." "His house is a pigsty." "She lets them watch too much TV." Is there any way to resolve all these differences?

Susan may have been justified in her anger over the girls' disappointment. Robert may have made an honest mistake. However, neither has much chance of changing the other, least of all by shouting and arguing.

Effective communication can help a great deal. Still, the only life a single parent can control is his own. Trying to manipulate the other parent or to force changes in attitudes and methods is likely to produce only resentment and anger—a loaded situation for the child caught in the middle.

It's undeniably painful for a child to deal with the disappointment caused by an irresponsible parent. Still, all of us must learn to handle disappointments and to accept reality, and you can help by focusing on the child's feelings rather than on the other parent's failures. Work on making your own home a secure and healthy place. When necessary, talk with your children—without blaming—about why you do things differently than their other parent. When conflicts and disappointments arise, acknowledge their feelings and explain your own. Sometimes a family meeting can help you find solutions to a problem.

New Habits for Old: Learning to Make It Work

Former mates *can* work together, but no one ever said it would be easy. A legal divorce is not enough—an "emotional divorce" is necessary before you can really change the old patterns of relating to your former spouse and begin to build a working relationship. Unfortunately, an emotional divorce — which includes recovery and healing from the trauma of separation — can take a long time. Adults who have experienced a divorce grieve, just like adults who have lost a mate to death. Sometimes it can seem that the grieving takes even longer, because the "lost" person is still out there and you still must cope with seeing him or her and, if you share children, having regular contact.

There are a number of events that can trigger a "relapse" during the emotional healing process. Things like having the divorce become final, celebrating holidays alone, or watching a former spouse remarry, buy a new home, or have a new child can cause the old wounds to reopen, both for you and for your children. Healing takes place in stages, but with each completed stage you move closer to true wholeness.

The house was quiet as Barbara washed her face and got ready for bed. She opened the windows to let in the cool evening breeze and checked the doors before going into ten-year-old Abigail's room to tuck her in. When Barbara got close to the bed, however, muffled sniffling sounds let her know that her daughter wasn't asleep after all.

"What's wrong, Abby?" Barbara asked gently, settling herself on the edge of the bed and stroking her daughter's hair. "I thought you were asleep. Do we need to have a cuddle and a talk?"

"Oh, Mom," Abby sighed and sat up. "I want to talk to you, but I don't know how."

"Well, honey," Barbara responded, "whatever it is, I'd like to help. Why don't you just tell me what's going on?"

There was a long, long pause. Barbara could feel her daughter gathering her courage. Finally, out came the news.

"Dad's getting married, Mom. Next month, to Joan. I get to be a bridesmaid with Cassie, Joan's daughter, and we get to go on the honeymoon and everything. I mean, it'll be fun and I'm happy for Dad. And I really like Joan and Cassie a lot and I've always wanted a sister. We're going to get a new house and Cassie and I will have our own rooms. But, Mom, it'll never be just Dad and me now—someone else will always be there. Everything's going to change. And if I want to spend more time with Dad and Joan, you'll be all alone and I *hate* that. Maybe you should get married, too. Oh, Mo-om!" And Abigail, overwhelmed, sniffled again, laying her head on her mom's shoulder.

Barbara was stunned. She didn't know how to respond. She was glad Dan had found someone as great as Joan and part of her was genuinely happy for them. The other part, though, felt as though it had just been kicked in the stomach—hard. She took a long, deep breath. The divorce had not been her choice and it had taken her a long time to feel even as good as she did now.

"Mom?" Abigail asked. "Are you okay?"

Barbara shook herself back to reality and looked into her daughter's face. "Yes, I'm okay. It just feels odd to think of your dad marrying someone else—I guess it still hurts a little. That surprises me. I knew your dad and Joan would marry one of these days and I didn't think I'd mind. But I know you really like Joan and Cassie and they've been great to you. If you decide you want to start spending more time at your dad's house, you know I will miss you, but I'm sure we can work it out.

"As for leaving me alone, Abby," Barbara continued, giving her daughter a squeeze, "I'll always have my precious little girl, no matter where you happen to be. And you know I really like my life these days— I have good friends and I love my work. I'd like to get married some day, but not any time soon. I'm just fine on my own, honey, and you don't need to worry about me. Now, you'd better get some sleep. Feel better?"

Abigail answered her mother with a wan smile and a hug, then burrowed down into the covers. Barbara lay awake a long time that night, thinking and remembering, and a few tears squeezed their way out. She realized it was going to be harder than she'd thought to watch Dan remarry, and to see Abby become part of a family in which Barbara had no place. She knew she'd be hearing a lot of wedding talk, and that she'd probably have to help with the bridesmaid's dress and that she probably wouldn't enjoy it much.

But Barbara also realized that just as she'd adjusted to Dan's leaving, she would adjust to his remarriage. And she'd been honest with Abby: she *did* like her life these days, and she never would have believed that was possible, even a year before.

"I'm going to make it," she told herself before she dropped off to sleep. "It's going to be different and I may have to grit my teeth a little, but I'm going to make it."

Being able to accept her ex-husband's remarriage, even though it was painful, meant the chances were good that Barbara would eventually be able to build a different sort of relationship with Dan, one in which they were working partners in raising their daughter. Slowly but surely, their old relationship was turning into something new, something that would eventually help their family to heal and change.

What About the "Old" Family?

It can take time to learn new patterns and responses. Ex-spouses are sometimes bewildered to find themselves addressing each other as "honey" or "dear" out of sheer habit, and other habits can linger as well. Other members of the "old" family — grandparents, aunts, uncles, cousins — often struggle to adjust to a divorce, too, and wonder how they'll fit into the new arrangements. Family members sometimes take sides, and a divorcing parent may cut children off from contact with the family of the former spouse.

It may be difficult — after all, it hurts to be excluded from "family" events — but try to keep in mind that your children will probably still consider themselves part of the "old family" and will still want to see Grandma and Grandpa, Aunt Kate and Uncle Bill.

What's more, those extended-family members may provide valuable support and relief for you, especially when everyone has begun to heal. Grandparents and other family members can be an important link between children and their history, and can provide a sense of permanence and continuity when everything else seems to have been shaken. It may be well worth the effort to keep those relationships alive and strong.

Communicating Effectively

Perhaps the single most positive thing ex-spouses can do to build a working relationship after divorce is to learn to communicate effectively. You can learn to communicate effectively even if your ex-spouse doesn't. Emotional honesty (see Chapter 2) does not require expertise from two people — one is enough. You can share what you think, what you feel, and what you want. The key is not expecting anyone else to think the same, to feel the same, or to give you what you want. Expressing yourself honestly is an important key to healthy self-esteem and healthy relationships. The next step is to decide what *you* will do (and to follow through), even when you can't control what someone else will do.

Some ex-spouses find it helpful to view their new relationship as a sort of partnership in the business of raising children, as Barbara hoped to do. It's possible to work through the details of visitation, and to share information on sports activities, school, illnesses, and special events, without referring to the emotional issues surrounding the end of the marriage.

Former spouses can learn to be accepting and considerate of each other's feelings, and to avoid actions they know will cause conflict. They can talk about parenting ideas; as we've suggested, they can even agree to take parenting classes in order to develop similar approaches. It may help to treat your former spouse as you would treat a co-worker. Keep your emotions in check and concentrate on getting the job done. Remember that good business associates are courteous and kind, but that they do expect agreements to be kept and are willing to follow through when necessary. They're also occasionally able to give others the benefit of the doubt.

It can seem impossible to work through problems, to lay aside past hurts and resentments, and to communicate effectively with an ex-spouse. Yet learning to do these things is the most important way to develop the "amicable relationship" we discussed earlier.

It may not be easy—in fact, there may be times when it seems downright impossible. It's sometimes helpful—or even necessary—to have the help of a good counselor or mediator. The point is that children deserve the chance to know and love both parents. They're healthier when they have that opportunity and the freedom to enjoy it.

When Children "Work the System"

Sooner or later, in single-parent households the world over, it happens. It's the ultimate threat against a single parent, and children figure it out with alarming speed. "I want to go live with my dad (or my mom)," they say. "I don't want to live with you anymore." It's a rare parent who can hear those words without feeling hurt and alarm.

Why do kids say that? They almost all do, eventually. Children are intelligent people and they do what works—and threatening to leave works so well because single parents love their children and often feel insecure, especially when the situation is new. Remember the mistaken goals? A child who threatens to go and live with his other parent may be acting out of a desire for revenge. He may feel hurt for some reason and may want to strike back at the nearest available person who cares — his parent. Or he may be threatening to leave as part of a power struggle. Kids often play their parents one against the other to get something they want even when their parents are married, and the ploy becomes far more effective when those parents are separated. Or the need may be real—a child may have compelling reasons for wanting to live with his other parent. It may even be your child's way of telling you that he just needs to spend more time with the other parent.

How can you tell what's really going on? A quick review of the Mistaken Goal Chart (pages 72-73) will help. If you can figure out how *you* feel when your child threatens to leave, you'll have an important clue to what's really going on. Using reflective listening and emotional honesty to talk through the problem will probably help you and your child resolve it peacefully. Try not to overreact. In fact, many times when a parent refuses to take the bait and responds by saying simply (and without anger or sarcasm), "Well, that may be something we should talk about," the threat loses some of its magic and the child retreats from it.

Melinda's initial response was to feel hurt when her 11-year-old son David announced, "I want to go live with Dad." Then she remembered the discussion on this very subject that had taken place two weeks ago in her single parenting class. She calmly said, "I'd like to discuss this with you later this evening."

David shot back, "You aren't going to change my mind."

Melinda said, "My goal is not to change your mind but to really hear and respect your thoughts and feelings, and I know I'll do a better job of that in a few hours. How about seven-thirty tonight?"

David agreed sullenly.

At 7:30 Melinda sat down at the kitchen table with David and began the conversation by saying, "I'm ready to listen to what's going on for you."

David said, "I just want to go live with Dad."

"I understand that," said Melinda, "and I'm not saying you can't. I would like to know what's behind it. Why do you want to go live with your dad?"

"I just do, that's why," David said.

Melinda said, "David, I have a hunch you feel hurt about something. I've tried to think what I might have done to hurt your feelings, but I don't have a clue. Is there something you aren't telling me?"

David started to cry. "I just miss my dad. Scott's dad is taking him camping this summer, and I hardly ever see my dad."

Melinda put her arms around David. "Oh, honey," she said. "I'm so sorry. I know how tough this can be. I know how much you love your dad. And the truth is, I can see why you'd want to be with him just as much as you're with me. At least I hope you still want to be with me too."

David admitted, "I do, but I just hate it that you and Dad got a divorce."

Melinda said, "I know, honey. Sometimes I hate it too. Life gives us some tough lessons to learn, but I know you and I get through this and also enjoy all the good stuff in life. I'll make a deal with you. You can try living with your dad for awhile. And if you change your mind and want to come back and live with me, that's okay. What you can't do is change your mind every time things get tough. You have two chances coming, so think about them carefully."

David asked, "Do you mean you wouldn't be mad at me if I lived with Dad for awhile?"

Melinda answered, "I'd miss you terribly, but I wouldn't be mad."

David did decide to live with his dad for a year. Then he decided to come back and live with his mother. Many single parents wouldn't want to consider the option of letting their children make choices about where they live, but it worked for Melinda. Several factors made it a workable option for her:

1. She was wise enough to wait through a "cooling-off" period before discussing such a "hot" issue.

2. Melinda knew (from her single parenting class and from the discussion of mistaken goals) that David probably wasn't aware that hurt feelings were motivating his actions. David didn't know he was feeling hurt. He'd confused the issue by covering up his

hurt feelings with anger—a common practice for many of us. His confusion led to actions of hostility: he struck back at the handiest person—his mom. Melinda's goal was to help him sort out his feelings and come to some kind of resolution.

3. Melinda was willing to be more concerned about her son's feelings than about her own. (Actually, she used her feelings to give her a clue that David might be feeling hurt even if it didn't make sense to her or to him initially.)

4. Melinda was willing to respect David's ability to make some decisions, but declared limits so David would make his decisions thoughtfully instead of reactively.

Many parents don't even consider the wishes of their children, and instead fight over children as though the parents' wishes were all that counted. Melinda encouraged David to love both his parents instead of feeling he was disloyal if he wanted to be with both (which, in this case, meant taking turns for awhile).

Melinda allowed David some choices. In other situations, just allowing a child to air his feelings is enough. Not everything requires "fixing" or resolutions. Often it's enough just to have a sensitive discussion, in which children can become more aware of their feelings and express them. This can start a process of healing and/or natural resolution.

When parents consider the thoughts and wishes of their children, they'll know that sometimes both parents are needed in the same place at the same time. If your child is lucky enough to have the love and active involvement of his other parent, that person will be a part of *your* life as long as you share your child. Your child will want to see both of you at school programs, Little League games, Girl Scout meetings, graduations, weddings—all of the important events and celebrations of life. Investing the time and energy to make your relationship with your child's other parent a positive and healthy one (even if it can't be a loving one) will spare you and your children a great deal of pain, and may lay the foundation for a happier, healthier life for all of you.

CHAPTER 12

Celebrating Your Family

It seems odd, but often the hardest person to convince that a single-parent family can be a whole family is the single parent him- or herself! All of us have acquired some firm ideas over the years about what families should be. When you ask most people what a normal family is, they'll tell you "normal" means a mom, a dad, and a couple of kids — no divorces, no remarriages, no complications. Even though that sort of family is now the exception rather than the rule, our expectations haven't kept up with the times. When you're a single parent — or a kid living in a single-parent home — it sometimes feels as if your family isn't quite right somehow. It may not be what you wanted for yourself and your children; it just doesn't look or feel like "Leave It to Beaver" or "The Cosby Show."

If you have read this far, you're probably starting to realize that single-parent homes can be wonderful places to grow up. Single-parent families are just that: *families*. A family is a circle of people who love each other, and they come in all shapes and sizes these days. Single-parent families are just one variation. They take some getting used to, but they can be peaceful, secure, loving homes for the adults and young people who share them.

Recognizing the Worth of Your Single-Parent Family

The first—and possibly the most important—thing you can do for your single-parent family is simply to recognize its worth and uniqueness. Both as individuals and as a family, you and your children have strengths, abilities, and perceptions that no one else has. Your family may not look or function quite like the one next door (or the one you see each week on television), but it's just as valuable.

It's often easier to focus on what's wrong than on what's right, but there's much that is positive about single-parent families. As we've said before, there's less chance of disagreement and conflict over parenting approaches, and many single parents report that they enjoy more time with their children, as well as the ability to be more spontaneous.

Remember, it may take time before we can find the blessings in single parenthood, but there are a number of ways to widen our vision, and to turn what seems negative into positive opportunities.

What's So Special About Our Family?

Human beings are wonderful creatures. Each of us is unique, possessing a special combination of qualities, insights, and abilities that no one else has. And because each of us is so special, the families we make are special as well. When you first find yourself a single parent, you may dwell on the things that are more difficult than they used to be, or things that appear to be different from what you see in "traditional" families. But as life settles down a bit, you'll be able to use your own wisdom and creativity to make some changes—perhaps not in the facts of your existence, but in the way you perceive them and in what you make of them.

One day soon, take time with your children, grab a big sheet of paper, and start thinking, talking, and writing down the things that make your family special. "We're not special at all," you may be saying. "We're just ordinary people trying to get by." But you'll find, if you take the time and energy to explore it, that there are some wonderful things that set your family apart.

What you discover may surprise you. There may be a special atmosphere of warmth and acceptance in your home, or a feeling of drive and enthusiasm. Each child has interests — baseball, soccer, ballet, video games, reading — that make him or her come alive. You have your own abilities and talents. Your family may have funny pets or shared interests (such as camping, biking, or gardening) that give you a sense of identity. Your home, your neighborhood, everything about you — even the uncomfortable parts — make you different and special.

Once you've filled your sheet of paper, spend some time together cutting out pictures from old magazines that illustrate the things you've written down. Then post your "family portrait" in a prominent place and add to it as inspiration strikes you. You may even find that there's a family motto or saying that will make a perfect title. Setting time aside, as a family, to discover what makes you special will help give you all a sense of unity and appreciation for what you have — and it will help you to see that your family's differences may be its greatest strengths.

Building New Traditions

A great deal of a family's identity and "specialness" lies in its traditions — the ways we spend our special times, the celebrations and rituals we build into our lives together. For single parents, holidays can be an especially difficult time. Time with the children often must be divided between parents, and for a single parent alone on a holiday or birthday, life can seem pretty bleak.

Many times the traditions and celebrations we've relied on in the past no longer feel right once we're single. Holidays are stressful for just about all families these days, and seem especially so for families complicated by divorce, death, or remarriage. Which set of parents do we spend the day with? How many turkey dinners will we have to eat? Whose children will be with which parents? Sometimes it seems that no matter how we choose to spend those special days, someone's feelings are bound to be hurt and someone is going to feel left out. Add to all of the above a liberal helping of financial stress and it's no wonder that single parents often find the prospect of holidays a depressing one.

There are a few things you can do to put the joy back in holidays and family occasions.

1. **Adjust your expectations to fit your situation.** Most of us still believe that family celebrations should resemble a Norman Rockwell painting. You know the one — Dad carves the huge, succulent turkey on a table set with beautiful things, while the family, rosy-cheeked and smiling, sits in happy anticipation. There are no arguments, no tired, whining children, no bitter memories. Unfortunately, reality is seldom like that, even for the happiest of families. Perhaps the best way to approach family traditions is to accept what *is*, and to make it the best it can be for everyone concerned.

2. **Don't be afraid to improvise or to do things differently.** It's hard not to fall for the "But we've always done it that way" approach, but don't be afraid to change what you do to fit who you are. If your children won't be with you on the "real" holiday, plan a special celebration for a day when you *are* together. There's nothing magical about the calendar — what matters is taking the time to create special moments together.

At first glance, some of your old traditions may

appear to be in tatters. If half of your cherished Christmas ornaments went with your ex-spouse, spend a day with your children making new ones. Bits of ribbon and construction paper, old Christmas cards, blown-out egg shells, photographs, and a little imagination will not only fill the empty spaces on your tree, but can create treasures you and your family will cherish for years to come — and some wonderful memories to go along with them.

3. **Ask your family what's most important to them, and build your celebrations around the answers.** It can be interesting to ask children which traditions mean the most to them. You may discover that no one particularly cares about the extravagant desserts you've been laboring over for years, but that everyone would enjoy time spent together playing a game or watching a special movie together. Don't be afraid to keep things simple — you may find that the best part of your special day is a walk together in the park after dinner.

   Your local bookstore or library is a good place to look for ideas — there are a number of excellent books on creating family celebrations. Whatever you and your family decide, spending time making special memories will help you build a sense of completeness and joy.

4. **Try to resist the pressure to give an abundance of gifts.** Don't confuse love with showers of presents. No one will enjoy a holiday if you're going to spend the ensuing months worrying about how to pay the bills. Remember that even two-parent families have children who say, "Is this all?" after they've opened a mountain of gifts. Instead of feeling guilty that you can't provide so many gifts, take this opportunity to teach your children other possibilities.

   You might want to give each child one special gift and use whatever money remains in your budget to help someone else, perhaps to "adopt" another family together. Amazing as it may seem sometimes, there are always people who are struggling more than we are. Finding a way to help someone else can both restore your perspective on what holidays are really about, and provide your children with valuable opportunities to share and to give.

New Ways to Celebrate

Finding new ways to celebrate holidays and to bind a single-parent family together can take courage. Ellen was dreading the prospect of Thanksgiving. Not only was it the first holiday since her divorce, but her two children would be spending the weekend with their father and grandparents, eating the usual turkey dinner with all of the family—except Ellen. The idea of sitting alone in her empty apartment brought tears to her eyes, but she wasn't sure what to do about it.

She was reading a magazine article about the Pacific Coast when an idea struck her, and she picked up the phone and made reservations before she could change her mind. That evening, Ellen and her children sat down together to make some plans.

"You two know that you'll be spending Thanksgiving with your dad and your grandparents this year, don't you?" Ellen asked. The children nodded, unsure how their mom was going to react.

Ellen smiled. "I still want to have a celebration with you even though we won't be together on Thanksgiving itself, so I thought we could have a special meal together on Wednesday, just us. What do you think?"

Enthusiastic smiles greeted the suggestion, and Ellen and her children planned a wonderful Thanksgiving together. The kids decided that since they'd be having turkey at their grandmother's house, they'd prefer cheeseburgers with Mom. Ellen laughed and agreed. Together they made a centerpiece with candles and Indian corn, talking while they worked about what the holiday meant. When their own "Thanksgiving" arrived, they set the table with the best dishes, lit the candles, and turned out the lights.

In the soft glow of the candles, Ellen took her children's hands and asked what each of them was thankful for. It took some time to think—it had been a difficult year for everyone — but each member of the family had at least one thing to be genuinely thankful for.

Then Benny, the youngest, asked uncertainly, "Can we say what we're not thankful for?" Ellen nodded at her son.

"I'm not thankful for the divorce," Benny said quietly, "but I'm glad we still love each other." More than one tear fell at the table that evening, but it was a time for healing and understanding as well, and Ellen knew as she hugged her children goodnight that their special "Thanksgiving" had been a good idea.

The next day, after Ellen had dropped her excited children off at their father's house, she packed a suitcase and drove off to the coastal town where she'd made reservations at a small bed-and-breakfast. It wasn't easy being alone. Still, she found she enjoyed the peace and quiet, having time to read a book and walk along the beach—and being somewhere new and interesting took the sting out of her rearranged holiday. In fact, she decided to take the children with her next year—her turn—for Thanksgiving at the beach. It was a beautiful spot, Ellen thought. Why not try something new?

Creating Special Moments

The moments that make us a family needn't be saved just for holidays and special occasions. Special "together" moments can happen every day—and it's important that we make time for them in our busy lives.

A neighbor looking in through the window of Brad's house might decide life there was a bit unusual. Brad comes home each night to three hungry children. There's usually laundry to do, homework to supervise, and all the little odds and ends that make up domestic life to take care of.

But Brad's approach is a little different. He walks through the front door, takes off his shoes, and stretches out on the carpet. "Where are my kids?" he shouts. "Where are all my children?"

And from wherever they happen to be, in the yard or in the house, Brad's children come running to throw themselves on their father's stomach, tickling, giggling, and shouting. For a while, it's a free-for-all. Then, when the laughter has subsided, Brad and his children talk about what's happened that day, how they're all feeling, and what lies ahead for the evening. It may seem like a silly ritual to the neighbors, but for Brad's family it's a wonderful way to stay in touch, and to make some time for laughter. Then they all tackle dinner and the chores together.

Special moments can be built around any activity that the family enjoys. Regular family meetings not only provide time to solve problems, but they build a sense of family and wholeness as each person participates and shares. Family meetings also teach that the single-parent family *works*, and they provide a time for listening, talking, and just having fun.

Creating special moments for your family may include such things as taking turns reading aloud from a book each evening before bed, taking a weekend bike ride, having a picnic or a baseball game, or simply hanging out together. These times need not be perfect—in fact, they probably won't be. But the more often they happen, the more solid a foundation your family will become for all of its members. The special moments you spend with your children need not cost a lot of money or be major events— time spent together simply *being* together is the most important thing.

One of the most valuable things parents can give their children is memories of times shared. These precious memories are the roots from which the family tree grows. And for single parents, special moments are a way to bind the family together, to heal, and to bring joy.

The Power of Ritual

There doesn't seem to be much time in modern life for rituals. In fact, most of us aren't really sure what the word means. Yet the weaving of ritual into our everyday existence can bring with it a richness and a sense of celebration that can make our lives joyful, at least most of the time!

Rituals are those familiar, repeated events that become part of the structure of our lives. Sometimes they simply happen on their own, but sometimes we can plan them, create them, and use them to gather and bind our family together. One familiar — and extremely effective — example is the bedtime ritual. Getting children to bed, especially young children, often becomes a nightly struggle that everyone in the family dreads. Developing a ritual allows children to feel secure and cozy and makes the entire process much easier.

For instance, bedtime should be consistent. You may decide to begin the process at 7:30, helping your toddler brush his teeth, wash up, and get into his pajamas. You might then settle down together in a favorite chair to read a special book, something soothing and cozy like *Goodnight Moon* or *Pat the Bunny*, or you may allow your child to pick one book himself. You may carry your child around his room to say good night to all his special toys and things, and perhaps say a prayer together. A hug, a kiss, and a loving "Sweet dreams," and the light goes out. Repeating this ritual every night can turn bedtime from a battle into a loving, enjoyable event.

Rituals can help us mark and celebrate the transitions and landmarks in our lives. They can help us heal, and give us a way to express sorrow or joy. Most of us are familiar with birthday rituals — the cake, the candles, the familiar song — but there's more you can do to make the occasion special. You may choose to take the birthday child out for a special "just us" lunch. Perhaps the birthday child will get to choose the dinner menu, and eat from a special plate. There may be an old, cherished decoration that *always* goes on the cake. One mom wraps small coins and a lucky charm in wax paper and puts them in the frosting between cake layers—the person who receives the lucky charm gets to make a special wish. If your child is adopted, celebrating the day he or she came to live with you can be a wonderful way to cement the bond between you.

If your children have lost a parent or a sibling through death, you may want to begin a special "ritual of remembering" on the anniversary of his or her death. You may choose to plant a tree or a rose, to look through old picture albums, or simply to share favorite memories over a special meal. Especially in those first difficult years, such rituals give your entire family an opportunity to share their sorrow, to remember, and to heal.

Rituals are a powerful way to bind a family together. Be sure, though, that you consider the uniqueness and the situation of your family when you plan these special celebrations of life. Though inherited or traditional celebrations can be wonderful events in the life of a family, doing something just because it's expected may create a sense of obligation and boredom rather than the spirit of identity and joy you're looking for. Make an effort to fit your rituals into your real life as a family; make them personal and special. Incorporating ritual into everyday life can give your entire family a chance to touch, to hope, and to celebrate.

Letting the Message of Love Get Through

It's all too easy for parents—all parents—to get caught up in the rush of daily life. We're busy *doing*, dealing with problems, listening, talking, keeping our families together. Sometimes we forget to take the time—or we're not sure how—to remind our children that we love them.

"Oh, my kids know I love them," most parents will say. "I tell them so all the time." But did you know that just saying the words is often not enough? Some interesting studies have shown that what communicates love most powerfully isn't what we say, but what we *do*: making eye contact, touching in affectionate ways, spending time together. Ruffling a son's hair as we pass by the chair where he's studying, or giving an unexpected hug to a daughter as she dutifully does the dishes, says "I love you and I appreciate you" in a wonderful way. Saying "yes" instead of "no" occasionally, especially when it's least expected, can delight children and make everyone feel more cheerful. Even the most inexpensive treat (a pack of gum, some baseball cards) takes on magic when it's given just to say "You're special."

A song from the movie "Mary Poppins" tells us that "a spoonful of sugar helps the medicine go down." The hassles of daily life with our children can seem less bitter and overwhelming when we manage to communicate love in the midst of them. We may find it necessary to use some positive discipline methods when our children have made unfortunate choices, but we can still smile or give an affectionate touch that says "You're my child and I still love you."

Some families find that a nonverbal signal, such as pointing to the heart, can express love and reassurance even during the most heated "discussion." Whatever works best for you and your family, be sure you take the time to let the message of love get through—it can make all the difference in the world.

One of the best (and healthiest) ways of expressing love and togetherness is through laughter. It's sometimes easier said than done, but nurturing your sense of humor, learning to recognize and enjoy the ridiculous in life, and finding ways to laugh with your children can make an astonishing change in how life *feels* for all of you.

Pete was giving his wilted petunias a shot of water one summer evening when Tyler and Travis, his twin sons, wandered out into the front yard. "We're bored, Dad," they moaned. "There's nothing to do and it's too hot in the house. And we don't want to go to bed—it's still light." Both boys flopped onto the front porch with perfectly matched frowns.

Pete felt a flash of annoyance. They'd already had this same conversation at least twice this week. They'd brainstormed about things to do, and they'd agreed to purchase a fan when there was enough money in the budget, yet here they were, at it again. He was looking over at his sons with irritated words on the tip of his tongue, when the sight of the two identical grumpy faces struck him as funny.

"Here," he said with a grin, "this might cool you down." And he gave the boys' bare legs a squirt with the garden hose.

Both boys leaped up with indignant squawks. "Da-ad!" they shrieked, running into the house and slamming the door behind them. "Oh, great," Pete thought. "Now I've gotten them mad." He was just getting ready to turn off the hose and go inside to talk to the boys when Travis and Tyler appeared around the corner of the house—armed to the teeth with their high-powered squirt guns.

For the next 15 minutes, the neighbors were treated to the sight of a pitched battle in Pete's front yard. And by the time the combatants finally collapsed in a heap on the grass, all three of them were soaked to the skin.

"Well," Tyler said soberly, looking down at his dripping T-shirt. "I guess I'm not hot anymore." Something in his voice tickled his brother and his father, and all three began to laugh, trooping into the house together for showers and bed.

Josie and her three children decided to have an ongoing contest in their family to see who could be the first to find the humor in a situation. The ground rule was that it had to be the kind of humor that would get them laughing "with" each other, not "at" each other. One day, as the family was returning from a picnic, Josie was stopped by a policeman for speeding and was given a ticket. She felt very upset about the fine she'd have to pay. One of her children quipped, "Well, Mom, you're always telling us mistakes are wonderful opportunities to learn. You just got a wonderful opportunity." Another child added, "Hey, that's right! And that policeman may have saved our lives by teaching you to slow down. That ticket may be a small price to pay for our lives." Josie chimed in, "Well, I'm always going to workshops for personal growth. It looks like I just provided us with a free private seminar. Now I won't have to lecture you guys about slowing down, because I just demonstrated the consequences." They all laughed — and learned.

Josie and her children also decided to make a cartoon scrapbook. They all scanned newspapers and magazines and cut out their favorite cartoons and pasted them in the scrapbook. They closed each family meeting by sharing the latest additions to the scrapbook. Every member of this family developed an excellent sense of humor.

Will laughter solve all of your problems? Of course not — but it certainly does make them seem less overwhelming. It's important to realize that there's a difference between shared laughter and ridicule. You'll know, if you listen to your inner wisdom, when laughter is positive and when it's hurtful.

Using your sense of humor and a little creativity can take the hassle out of much of daily life. A spontaneous pillow fight or tickling match, or making a funny face at an unexpected moment, can remind parents and children alike that life can still be pretty wonderful — even when there are chores to do. Sometimes a child who balks at picking up toys will hurry to do it when it becomes a game. Sometimes a smile and a "Bet you can't pick up those toys (or put on your pajamas or brush your teeth) by the time I count to ten" make the task an occasion for fun rather than consequences. And sometimes just trading jokes and silly stories gives everyone an opportunity to smile together, something that doesn't happen nearly enough in most of our homes.

Sometime when you have a quiet moment, think back on your own childhood and see what it is that you most enjoy remembering—or what you wish you had to remember. Will your children have laughter, celebrations, and other good times to look back on? Creating those special times is easier (and less expensive) than you might think. It can actually become a way of life, and it can transform the atmosphere in your home. Making space for ritual, tradition, laughter, and shared memories will make your family *feel* like a family, and will help you create a home where people want to come and stay a while.

None of us gets to choose all of the circumstances of our lives. There's an old cliché that tells us, "Into each life some rain must fall," and for some of us life seems to have been a veritable flood! But there's another cliché, tired but still true, that tells us "When life hands you lemons, make lemonade!" Whether or not being a single parent was your choice, your family is your family. It will be whatever you have the courage to make it. Believe in your heart that it can be something wonderful, take whatever steps you can, and celebrate!

Conclusion

Well, then, where do we find ourselves now? We've come to the end of a book, but it's only the beginning of a journey. Single parenthood may be a trip you never wanted to take, and you may still find it frightening, confusing, overwhelming. Or you may be realizing that like most trips, this one will have some rough spots but will hold some wonderful moments as well.

Parenting is almost always more of a learning experience for the parent than for the child, and single parenthood offers special opportunities for growth and change. Both adults and children may approach it reluctantly — often both are shattered and hurting. But at its best, single parenthood is the chance to put the shattered pieces back together and to build something beautiful from them.

Yes, it *is* possible to raise responsible, respectful, resourceful children as a single parent. It's our hope as authors — and as parents — that you now possess some new skills and understanding that will help you reach that goal. Yes, it *is* possible to build a home that is secure, loving, and happy, a place where both adults and children can thrive and learn. Yes, we all realize it won't always be easy; but the rewards, for us and for our children, can be so great.

Being a single parent may be the hardest thing you ever have to do, but it's also undoubtedly the most important. You have the opportunity to give your children the qualities and abilities that will make them effective, healthy human beings, and to share the wonderful joy that their experience can bring. Single or not, you're first and foremost your children's *parent*.

Nothing you ever do will make as much of an impact on this world as the legacy you leave through your children.

Remember our cypress tree? If that tree could speak, it might tell us that there are times it wishes it were *anywhere* else, when hanging on to the rock takes more strength than the tree seems to possess. It may be tempting to give in to the wind and the storm, to simply let go.

But both the cypress tree and the single parent possess a strength that comes from the storm itself. They endure and they grow, and they provide shelter, beauty, and inspiration for those who gather beneath their branches. And when the sun breaks through, the sight is a wonder to behold.

Each single parent must eventually find his or her own way, learning to trust his or her own wisdom, to change when it seems right. Mistakes and discouragement are inevitable — but what truly matters is not where you are, but where you're going. None of us will ever be perfect parents; our children are unlikely to be perfect children. But if you're doing the best you can, making occasional mistakes but loving each other along the way, you'll know you're heading in the right direction. That's all any parent can ever do — and, yes, it's enough.

Index

About the Authors

Jane Nelsen, Ed.D. (far right), founder of Capable People Associates, is a popular lecturer and the author of several books on parenting. She has appeared on "Oprah," "Sally Jessy Raphael," "Twin Cities Live," and was the featured parent expert on the "National Parent Quiz," hosted by Ben Vereen. Jane is the mother of seven children and the grandmother of eleven.

Cheryl Erwin (far left) is the parenting education trainer for the Children's Cabinet, a nonprofit family resource center in Reno, Nevada. She graduated from the University of Texas with a degree in journalism and has been writing on parenting issues and teaching parenting classes for five years. Cheryl is a single mother who lives with her nine-year-old son, a cat, and a bird.

Carol Delzer, J.D., M.A. (center) is a family law attorney-mediator whose case load includes divorce and child-custody cases. She has a masters degree in family counseling and is a registered MFCC intern. She lives with her daughter, Jessica, who inspired her to help write this book.

For information on lectures, seminars, and leadership training workshops with Jane Nelsen or Cheryl Erwin, call 1-800-879-0812.

BOOKS AND TAPES BY JANE NELSEN

To: Sunrise Books, Tapes & Videos, Box B, Provo, UT 84603 Phone: 1-800-456-7770

BOOKS	Price	Quantity	Amount
POSITIVE DISCIPLINE FOR SINGLE PARENTS by Nelsen, Cheryl Erwin & Carol Delzer	$10.95	_____	_____
POSITIVE DISCIPLINE A-Z by Nelsen, Lynn Lott & H. Stephen Glenn	$14.95	_____	_____
POSITIVE DISCIPLINE IN THE CLASSROOM by Nelsen, Lott & Glenn	$14.95	_____	_____
RAISING SELF-RELIANT CHILDREN IN A SELF-INDULGENT WORLD by Glenn & Nelsen	$10.95	_____	_____
I'M ON YOUR SIDE by Nelsen & Lott	$9.95	_____	_____
POSITIVE DISCIPLINE by Nelsen	$9.95	_____	_____
TIME OUT by Nelsen & Glenn	$6.95	_____	_____
UNDERSTANDING by Nelsen	$9.95	_____	_____
CLEAN AND SOBER PARENTING by Nelsen, Riki Intner & Lott	$10.95	_____	_____

MANUALS	Price	Quantity	Amount
POSITIVE DISCIPLINE IN THE CLASSROOM FACILITATOR'S GUIDE by Nelsen, Lott and Glenn	$39.95	_____	_____
DEVELOPING CAPABLE PEOPLE MANUAL by Glenn and Nelsen			
Leader's Guide	$59.95	_____	_____
Participant's Workbook	$6.95	_____	_____
TEACHING PARENTING MANUAL by Lott and Nelsen	$39.95	_____	_____
EMPOWERING PARENTS OF TEENS by Nelsen, Lott, Beverly Berna & Ellen Spurlock	$24.95	_____	_____

CASSETTE TAPES	Price	Quantity	Amount
POSITIVE DISCIPLINE IN THE CLASSROOM by Nelsen (six-tape set)	$49.95	_____	_____
DEVELOPING CAPABLE PEOPLE by Glenn (six-tape set)	$49.95	_____	_____
EMPOWERING TEENAGERS AND YOURSELF IN THE PROCESS by Nelsen and Lott (seven-tape set)	$49.95	_____	_____
POSITIVE DISCIPLINE by Nelsen	$10.00	_____	_____

SUBTOTAL _____

UT residents add 6.25% sales tax; CA residents add 7.25% sales tax _____

Shipping & Handling: $2.50 plus 50" for each item _____

TOTAL _____

(Prices subject to change without notice.)

METHOD OF PAYMENT (check one):
_____ Check made payable to SUNRISE, INC. _____ Mastercard _____ Visa

Card #_____ _____ _____ _____ Expiration _____ / _____

Ship to_____

Address _____

City/State/Zip_____

Daytime Phone_____

For a free newsletter, call toll-free: 1-800-456-7770

For a free newsletter and information on
lectures and workshops by Jane Nelsen
call 1-800-456-7770.